D1523807

A Thousand Drifts of Snow

A Thousand Drifts of Snow

Ancient Chinese Poetry

Translated by

Kwan-Hung Chan

INFI∞ITY
PUBLISHING.COM

ISBN 0-7414-5644-3

Published by:

PUBLISHING.COM

1094 New DeHaven Street, Suite 100
West Conshohocken, PA 19428-2713
Info@buybooksontheweb.com
www.buybooksontheweb.com
Toll-free (877) BUY BOOK
Local Phone (610) 941-9999
Fax (610) 941-9959

Printed in the United States of America

Published May 2010

This book is dedicated to my parents

Cheuk-Fai Chan

And

Sau-Ying Yuen

Contents

Preface 1

1. ZHOU DYNASTY (1122-256 BCE)
BOOK OF SONGS (c600 BCE)
Bird Song 2
Quiet Girl 2
Peach Tree 3
Katydids 3

2. HAN DYNASTY (206 BCE-220 CE)
NINETEEN ANCIENT POEMS (206 BCE-220CE)
The Cowherd Star is Far, Far away 4
Green, Green Grass by the River 5
Walking On and On 5

3. SIX DYNASTIES (220-589)
WANG XIZHI (309-c365)
Orchid Pavilion 6
TAO QIAN (365-427)
Drinking Wine 6
Return to My Farm, no. 1 7
Return to My Farm, no. 5 7
XIE LINGYUN (385-433)
Beginning My Trip from Shiguan Pavilion at Night 8
Passing a Lake from the South Hill to the North Hill 8

ZHAN FANGSHENG (fl.400)
Sailing back to the Capital......................................9
Sailing into the South Lake 10

BAO ZHAO (c414-466)
Ascending Mount Lu....................................10

ANONYMOUS (c439-534)
The Ballad of Mulan.................................11

4. TANG DYNASTY (618-907)

SHEN CHUANQI (mid 7th century)
The Garrison at Huanglong 14

HE ZHIZHANG (659-745)
A Note on Homecoming...............................14
To Willow......................................14

CHEN ZIANG (661-702)
Climbing the Terrace of Yuzhou......................15

ZHANG JIULING (678-740)
Complaint, no. 2 15
Complaint, no. 4 15
Looking at the Moon and Longing for a Distant
    Lover..16

WANG ZHIHUAN (688-742)
Beyond the Frontier...............................16
Climbing the Pavilion of the Storks 17

MENG HAORAN (689-740)
Drinking at the Daoist Priest Mei's Hermitage 17
Feelings at the Beginning of Winter................17
In the South Pavilion on a Summer Day,
    Thinking of Xin the Elder......................18

Mooring at Night on the Tonglu River and
 Remembering an Old Friend at Guangling............. 18
Mooring on the River at Jiande 18
On Climbing Mount Xian with Some Friends............. 19
On Climbing Orchid Mountain in Autumn - a Poem
 for Zhang the Fifth........................ 19
On Returning to South Mountain at the Year's End 19
On Stopping at an Old Friend's Homestead................. 20
Parting from Wang Wei..................... 20
A Poem for Minister Zhang composed by Lake
 Dongting 21
Spring Dawn.................. 21
Written in the Qin Country, for a Buddhist Priest,
 Master Yuan 21

WANG CHANGLING (c690-756)
Complaint in the Palace of Loyalty 22
Going up to the Frontier 22
Passing the Frontier 22
Returning from the Frontier.............. 23

WANG WEI (701-761)
Autumn Night............... 23
Birdsong Torrent............... 23
Deer Park 24
Farewell 24
Farewell to Xin Jian at the Lotus Pavilion 24
Green Gully 24
The Hermitage of the Bamboos.............. 25
A poem for Commissioner Li before his Departure
 for Zizhou 25
My Retirement Villa by Mount Zhongnan 25
Remembrance 26
A Reply to Assistant Prefect Chang 26
Taking Leave of Ji Wuqian who has Failed the Official

Examination and is Returning to his Village 26
Thinking of my Brothers in Shandong on the Ninth
    Day of the Ninth Moon 27
A View of River Han 27
Written on Returning from Mount Song 28
The Zhongnan Range 28

LI BAI (701-762)

At a Banquet Held in Xie Tiao's Tower in Xuanzhou,
    to bid Farewell to Archivist Shu Yun 28
Bring in the Wine 29
Chanting on the River 30
Drinking alone under the Moon 31
Farewell to Meng Haoran for Guangling 32
For Meng Haoran 32
Going down to Jiangling 32
The Moon 32
The Moon at the Border 33
Night Thoughts 33
On Climbing Phoenix Tower at Jinling 33
On the Mountain: a Conversation 34
Pining 34
Resolutions after being Drunk on a Spring Day 34
Sending off a friend to the Kingdom of Shu 35
Toast with a Hermit 35
Lady Yang 35
Viewing the Waterfall of Mount Lu 36
A Visit to a Priest 36

DU FU (712-770)

Climbing on the Double Ninth Day 36
Dreaming of Li Bai 37
Gazing at the Great Mount 38
Moonlit Night 39

New Moon 39
On Leaving Marshall Fang's Tomb 40
Spring Prospect 40
Thinking of my Brothers on a Night of Moonlight 40
The Visitor 41

WANG HAN (fl. 713)
The Song of Liangzhou 41

CEN SHEN (715-770)
Climbing the Pagoda at Zien Monastery with
    Gao Shi and Xue Chu 42
On Meeting a Messenger Going to the Capital 43

GAO SHI (716-765)
Seeing off Assistant-Magistrate Li Degraded to
    Xiazhong and Assistant-Magistrate Wang
    degraded to Changsha 43

ZU YONG (early 8th century)
Looking at the Snow Drifts on South Mountain 43

LI QI (fl. 725)
An Old Theme 44
On Seeing Wei Wan off to the Capital 44

LU LUN (c748-c798)
Farewell to Li Duan 45

HAN HONG (mid 8th century)
Festival of Cold Food 45
A Reply to Cheng Jin's Poem, written in the Same
    Measure 45

JI WUQIAN (early 8th century)
Spring Boating on Reye Stream 46

LIU ZHANGQING (c719-c787)

Climbing to the Monastery on General Wu's Terrace
and Surveying the Prospect on an Autumn Day 46
Farewell to the Monk Ling Che 47
Looking for Chang, the Daoist Recluse of
South Stream 47
The Lute Player 47
On Seeing Wang the Eleventh Leave for the South 48
Written at New Year 48

YUAN JIE (719-772)

Addressed to my Officials and Subordinates after
the Retreat of the Rebels 48

DAI SHULUN (732-789)

On Meeting at an Inn an Old Friend from my Village
in Jiangnan 49

WEI YINGWU (737-c792)

Anchoring at Yu Yi in the Evening 50
A Farewell to Li Cao in the Rain 50
A Ferry West of Chuzhou 51
A Lucky Meeting on the River Huai with an
Old Friend from Liangzhou 51
On the Eastern Outskirts 51

LIU SHENXU (fl.742-755)

Poem 52

CUI SHU (d.739)

Climbing Wang Xian Terrace on the Double Ninth:
Presented to Vice-Prefect Liu 52

CUI HAO (d.754)

Passing Hua Yin 53
Yellow Crane Pavilion 53

ZHANG JI (mid 8th century)

Anchored at Night by Maple Bridge 54

LIU YUXI (772-842)

Black Gown Lane 54
Song of Bamboo Twigs 54
A Spring Song 54

BAI JUYI (772-842)

Song of Lasting Regret 55

LIU ZONGYUAN (773-819)

Living by a Brook 60
Morning Walk in Autumn 60
River Snow 60

YUAN ZHEN (779-831)

Elegy, no. 1 61
Elegy, no. 2 61
Elegy, no. 3 62

JIA DAO (779-843)

The Absent Hermit 62

LI SHEN (780-846)

"Old Style" 63

CUI HU (c796)

At a Homestead South of the Capital 63

LI SHE (fl.806)

Half-day Leisure in the Hills 63

ZHU QINGYU (early 9th century)

The Approaching Examination: for Zhang Ji 64
Within the Palace 64

LI YI (late 8th-early 9thcenturies)

Joy at Meeting a Cousin and saying Farewell again 65
Marching to Shouxiang at Night and Hearing a Pipe.... 65

LIU FANGPING (8th-9^{Tth} centuries)

Spring Bitterness.. 65

LIU ZHONGYONG (8th-9th centuries)

A Soldier's Complaint... 66

ZHANG HU (9th century)

Jiling Terrace, no. 1... 66
Jiling Terrace, no. 2... 66
To a Court Lady... 67
Written on the Wall of Jinling Ferry-House................... 67

DU QIUNIANG (early 9th century)

The Coat with the Gold Threads.................................... 67

DU MU (803-852)

Autumn Night... 67
Confession 68
Given in Farewell, no. 1 68
Given in Farewell, no. 2 68
Climbing Loyou Hill before Leaving for Wuxing.......... 68
Climbing Mount Qi on the Ninth Day of the
     Ninth Moon.. 69
For Assistant Prefect Han Chuo of Yangzhou.............. 69
Mooring on the Qinhuai River....................................... 69
For the Wu Jiang Pavilion 69
The Red Cliff... 70

WEN TINGYUN (812-870)

Complaint of a Jade Lute... 70
Ferrying South at Lizhou... 70
Su Wu's Temple 71

Taking Leave of a Friend Going East........................71
Dreaming of the South Side of the River 72

LI SHANGYIN (c813-858)
Ancient Zither..72
At Bei Jing Luo Monastery 73
At Choubi Post-House 73
Because… 74
The Cicada 74
Climbing Loyu Plateau 74
For the Official Ling Hu 75
Jasper Pool 75
Moon Lady 75
To… 75
Spring Rain 76
A Sui Dynasty Palace 76
Thoughts in the Cold 77
Untitled, no. 1 77
Untitled, no. 2 78
Untitled, no. 3 78
Wind and Rain 79

CHEN TAO (824-882)
Song of Long Si...79

WEI ZHUANG (836-910)
Despair 79
Impressions of Jinling.....................................80
Lovesickness 80
Night Thoughts at Zhang Tai..........................80
Yearnings 81

LI PIN (mid 9th century)
On Crossing the River Han...............................81

MA DAI (mid 9th century)
Autumn Hut by the River Ba 81
By the River Chu, Remembering the Past 82

CUI TU (late 9th century)
Reflections on New Year's Eve 82
The Solitary Wild Goose 83

DU XINHE (late 9th century)
Grievance in the Spring Palace 83

HAN WU (late 9th century)
Already Cool 83

QIN TAOYU (late 9th century)
The Poor Girl 84

ZHANG QIAO (late 9th century)
News from the Frontier 84

ZHANG BI (10th century)
For Someone 85

LI YU (937-978)
Court Dancer 85
Lament 86
Longings 86
Parting Grief 86
Regret 87
Sorrow 87
Woe 88
Yearnings 88
Upon Waking from a Dream 88

5. SONG DYNASTY (960-1279)

LIU YONG (987-1053)

Longings 89
Parting.. 89

OUYANG XIU (1007-1072)

Memory 90
Regret.. 91
West Lake 91
The Thrush.. 91

SU SHI (1037-1101)

Drunk again after Sobering up, by the East Slope......... 92
During the Mid-Autumn Festival 92
Memories of the Past at the Red Cliff 93
Caught in the Rain 94
Secret Love 94
Spring Night 95
To my Dead Wife 95
The West Lake when Rain is Falling............................ 96
Written on the Wall of Xilin Monastery....................... 96

QIN GUAN (1049-1110)

The Cowherd Star and the Weaver Maid 96
A Long, Cold Night.. 97

LI QINGZHAO (1081-1143)

Lady on a Swing 97
Autumn Festival 98
Flowers from a Peddler.. 98
Grief... 99
Fisherman's Pride 99
By the Brook.. 100
The Rain Last Night 100

Alone 100
Lantern Festival 101
Lament at Night 102
Longing for My Lover 102
Sorrow 103

ZHAO JI (r 1101-1125)
To Apricot Blossoms 103
To Swallows 104

YUE FEI (1103-1142)
The River Runs Red 104

LU YOU (1125-1210)
Ambition 105
Awakening 106
Complaint 106
Fisherman's Delight 107
Hearing the Cuckoo at Night 108
Instruction to My Son 108
My Faraway Hometown 109
My Philosophy of Life 109
To Plum Blossoms 110
Traveling by Boat along the Fan River 110
Unfulfilled Ambitions 110

XIN QIJI (1140-1207)
Looking for Her in the Lantern Festival 111
Written on the Wall in the Boshan Temple 112

6. YUAN DYNASTY (1280-1367)
JIANG JIE (1245-1310)
Listening to the Rain 112

MA JIYUAN (c1260-c1324)
Autumn Thoughts 113
GUAN DAOSHENG (1262-1319)
To My Husband 113

7. MING DYNASTY (1368-1644)

LIU XIAOZU (fl. 1550)
To My Lover 114
XUE LUNDAO (fl. 1580)
Angry at the World 114
Mr. Goody-Goody 115

8. QING DYNASTY (1644-1911)

NALAN XINDE (1655-1685)
Confession 116
Lament 116
Homesickness 116
A Listless Life 117
Loneliness 117
Sorrow 118
Wanderer's Woe 118

Index of Authors 119

Appendix: Chinese Texts 121

Preface

The title of this book is taken from the poem "Memory of the Past at the Red Cliff" by Su Shi (1037-1101). In 208, a decisive battle of the Three Kingdoms era was fought there. In the poem, he described the waves at the Red Cliff pounding the shore and rolling up like a thousand drifts of snow. I found joy, rewards and challenges translating this famous poem.

In this book, I have translated over two hundred and thirty well-known and important ancient Chinese poems from about seventy-five poets, dating from 600 BCE to the seventeenth century. For a balance of themes, I have excluded some poems from the Tang Dynasty, touching upon familiar and similar subjects already represented. Included instead are poems from some less-established poets of other dynasties, for their special messages.

The poets are presented in chronological order to show the development in style through the centuries. An author index with Pinyin transliteration is provided in alphabetical order, followed by the Chinese texts in an appendix.

I would like to thank all of my friends and relatives who have helped and encouraged me in this project.

BOOK OF SONGS (c600 BCE)

Bird Song

Ospreys sing and call,
On an isle at the riverside.
A gentle and graceful maiden,
For the lord, makes a fit bride.

Long and short Floating Hearts
Flow by, left and right.
A gentle and graceful maiden,
The lord seeks, day and night.

When courtship fails,
In bed or out, he yearns,
For a long, long while,
Making tosses and turns.

Long and short Floating Hearts
We pluck, left and right.
A gentle and graceful maiden,
Harp and lute to unite.

Long and short Floating Hearts
We choose, left and right.
A gentle and graceful maiden,
Drum and bell to delight.

Quiet Girl

The quiet girl is dainty,
At the corner, hiding in wait,
Loving but avoiding me.
Scratching my head, I hesitate.

The quiet girl is tender so.
A red tube she gives to me.
The red tube sheds a glow.
I am glad for a gift from a beauty.

From the pasture comes this weed,
But to me it is rare and pretty,
Only because you are beautiful, I heed,
And it is a gift from a beauty.

Peach Tree

Young and fresh like a peach tree,
With flowers sharp and bright.
Married this maiden will be.
For his house she is right.

Young and fresh like a peach tree,
With plump fruits in sight.
Married this maiden will be.
For his home she is right.

Young and fresh like a peach tree,
With lush leaves in sight.
Married this maiden will be.
For his family she is right.

Katydids

Katydids sing
And hop together.
Mine is a worried heart,
For from my man, I am apart.
But once we meet, eye to eye,
And my man I am nigh,

A soothed heart will be mine.

Yon south hills I climb.
Some ferns I gather.
Mine is an anxious heart,
For from my man, I am apart.
But once we meet, eye to eye,
And my man I am nigh,
A joyful heart will be mine.

Yon south hills I climb.
Some ferns I gather.
Mine is a grieving heart,
For from my man I am apart.
But once we meet, eye to eye,
And my man I am nigh,
A relieved heart will be mine.

NINETEEN ANCIENT POEMS (206 BCE-220CE)

The Cowherd Star is Far, Far away

The Cowherd Star is far, far away.
The bright Weaver Maid is by the Milky Way,
With her snow-white hands, soft and light,
Pulling the shuttle, good and tight.
The day is over, the work not so.
Her tears, like rain, flow.
Though clear and shallow is the Milky Way,
They will be apart for many a day.
Over the brimming waters, each other they seek.
Yet to each other, they do not speak.

Green, Green Grass by the River

Green, green grass by the river.
Lush, lush garden willows.
A graceful maiden in a tower
Brightly at the window shows.

A beauty with a rouge-powdered face,
And white, slender hands in display.
A singer for hire before,
She is a wanderer's wife today.

The wanderer has left and been long gone.
How hard it is to be with an empty bed alone.

Walking On and On

Walking on and on,
You left me and broke our tie,
Over myriad miles,
Each at one end of the sky.

With the long, blocked roads,
Of a reunion, none can know.
Tartar horses follow the north wind.
For south nesting branches, birds of Yue go.

Our parting gets longer each day;
My belt has become loose.
Floating clouds cover the sun.
To shy away, you choose.

Yearning for you ages me.
Many years have slipped away.
I give up and keep quiet.
Try to eat more every day.

WANG XIZHI (309-c365)

Orchid Pavilion

Upwards, I see the blue sky to its verge
And downwards, green waters to the rim.
All vistas are infinite, quiet and alone,
With a display of patterns, orderly and trim.

Magnificent is the Creator's work,
With myriad differences and none askew.
Since a flute plays with long or short pipes,
I find fitting in something new.

TAO QIAN (365-427)

Drinking Wine

My home is built in an urban area,
But the din of cart and horse, I do not find.
You ask, how can this be done?
This land seems remote through my far-reaching mind.

I pluck chrysanthemums by the east hedge.
There is good mountain air, day and night.
Restfully I view the South Mountain
And birds returning together in flight.

There is truth in what life is meant to be.
Before I can analyze it, words fail me.

Return to My Farm, no. 1

When young, I was not tradition-bound.
I preferred hills to worldly affairs.
By mistake, I have fallen into this net
Of social entanglements for thirty years.

Caged birds miss their old forests.
Fish in ponds long for their former depths still.
I plough some wasteland near the southern edge
And return to farming, though lacking skill.

Ten or more acres of fields surround the house.
Thatched huts number eight or nine.
Elms and willows shade the rear eaves.
Before the hall, peach and plum trees line.

Other villages are lost in the distance.
Hazy puffs of smoke from the hamlets show.
Dogs bark in the deep alleys.
Atop mulberry trees, chickens crow.

My home, free of dust, is uncluttered.
In the roomy space, I feel amply free.
Shut in a cage too long,
Back to nature, I now get to be.

Return to My Farm, no. 5

On a rugged road winding through the bushes,
I return with a single cane, feeling despondent.
The mountain stream, clear and shallow,
To wash my feet, can well be lent.

I heat some newly-brewed wine.
Then with a chicken cooked, my neighbors I invite.

At sundown, in my darkened room,
I have bramble wood for light.

The night is painfully short in our joy and fun.
Over to the next morn, time has already run.

XIE LINGYUN (385-433)

Beginning My Trip from Shiguan Pavilion at Night

I hike on myriad miles of hilly roads.
For ten evenings on a stream I float.
When birds return to their nests,
I rest my oars and boat.

Stars begin to thin out.
I call it a weary trip.
The dawn moon is still high and bright.
Chilly, morning dewdrops drip.

Passing a Lake from the South Hill to the North Hill

I start from the cliffs of the South Hill at dawn,
By sunset, on the peak of the North Hill, to recline.
I leave my boat for a view of the round islets,
Spurning my walking stick and leaning on a thick pine.

The side paths run long and narrow.
The islets look clear and bright.
I look down for the tips of tall trees
And hear from above the big gully's roaring might.

A rock blocks and diverts the stream.
In the dense forest, a trail cannot be traced.
The weather changes, but who can feel?
Luxuriant vegetation has surfaced.

The first bamboo-shoots are sheathed in green.
New reeds hold purple hair.
Seagulls sport on shores in spring.
Pheasants play in the wind, mild and fair.

The mind of Heaven on Earth is limitless.
My love for Nature's work goes deep.
I do not regret my distance from ancient people,
Only the dissimilar minds we may keep.

Emotional satisfaction is not just what a lonely trip brings.
When done, who understands Nature's scheme of things?

ZHAN FANGSHENG (fl.400)

Sailing back to the Capital

Towering mountains rise in great heights.
Long lakes for myriad miles stay clear.
White sands are clean all year long.
In winter or summer, green pine-groves appear.

Water never for a moment stops.
After a thousand years, wood keeps its integrity.
Waken, I compose a new poem.
My wanderer's woe suddenly leaves me.

Sailing into the South Lake

Lake Pengli joins three rivers.
Mount Lu towers over many a hill.
White sands make waterways clear.
Everywhere on the crags, green pines fill.

Since when did this water flow,
With this hill developed along?
Men's fate shifts in cycles.
Only these forms stay long.

Within the universe, through the distant past,
Ancient and present make first and last.

BAO ZHAO (c414-466)

Ascending Mount Lu

The waterscape is marred by the luggage we pole.
The trip ends in a hut by the hillside.
A thousand crags rise in blocks and piles.
Myriad valleys, in twists and turns, slide.

More impressing and majestic than before,
In confusion, a former name it goes by.
Cave streams show the veins of the earth.
Tall trees hide the meridians of the sky.

Pine bridges lead to a secluded maze above.
Cloud pockets hang low everywhere and stay.
In summer, ice in the shade stays frozen solid.
Some flaming trees flourish on a winter day.

Morning birds make their calls.
Night monkeys cry clear and loud.
Deep cliffs embed signs of Heaven's feat.
A lasting spirit, the sharp peak does shroud.

Driven by the nature of a mountain-lover
And the faraway traveler's delight,
We trek on the Daoist priest's path,
Forever with smoke and mists in sight.

ANONYMOUS (c439-534)

The Ballad of Mulan

I

Click, click, again, click, click.
The noise will never leave.
Facing the door, Mulan will always weave.
But the sound of the shuttle cannot fight
The loud sighs of Mulan in her plight.

II

Parents ask, "What is on your mind?
What is it you recall and find?"
Daughter replies, "Nothing is on my mind.
Nothing is there to recall and find.

I feel all right,
Except that I saw the draft lists last night.
For the many troops the Khan calls,
In each of the twelve lists, Father's name falls.

11

Father has no son who is grown.
Mulan has no older brother to call her own.
To buy a saddle and a horse is my will
And Father's post at war to fill."

In the East Market, she buys a horse, one of the best
And a saddle from the West.
In the South Market, she gets a bridle, and henceforth
A long whip from the North.

At dawn, to Parents she bids goodbye.
At dusk, by the Yellow River's bank, her camp does lie.
Her parents she cannot hear.
Only the rumble of the Yellow River is clear.

Then at dawn, to the Yellow River, she bids farewell.
At dusk on the Black Mountain, she stops to dwell.
Her parents she cannot hear,
Only the neighing of Mount Yen's nomad horses far and
        near.

On myriad miles of war and battle,
Army pots in the north wind rattle.
Over passes and hills as in flight,
Her iron armors shine in the cold light.

III

After a hundred battles, their demise generals may earn.
After ten years of war, brave soldiers may return.

On her return, she sees the Khan.
Seated in the Luminous Hall, he makes a plan
Of giving her promotions, rapid and grand,
And rewards of extensive land.

When the Khan asks for her needs,
Mulan replies and pleads,
"A minister I have no desire to be,
But to go home on a swift mount, please allow me."

Outside the city wall, Parents walk
As soon as they hear the talk
Of Daughter's return with no harm,
Helping each other by the arm.

When Elder Sister hears her younger sister will come
And Younger Brother knows his older sister will be home,
At the window, a fresh rouge-powdered face she wants to
        keep,
And he whets his cleaver swiftly, facing some pigs and
        sheep.

IV

The door to my east chamber, I open to probe.
My soldier's garb I start to disrobe.
In the west room, I get on a couch to sit
And put on clothes I used to fit.

At the window, my cloud-like hair I comb.
Then coming out to meet my comrades, I drop a bomb.
On my forehead, with the help of a mirror on the wall,
I have fixed a yellow petal, shocking them all.

For twelve years together, from many battles won,
That Mulan is a woman was known by none.
It is said male hares run with an unsure gait
And female hares do not look straight.

On the ground, two similar hares run side by side.
What gender is each? How can one decide?

SHEN CHUANQI (mid 7th century)

The Garrison at Huanglong

They say the guards at Huanglong
Have not been relieved for years in a row.
What a pity, the same moon for her chamber,
Upon the Han soldiers' camp, long sheds its glow.

In spring, a young wife instantly feels
The passion her husband had a previous night.
Who will lead the flags and drums
And capture Dragon City with his might?

HE ZHIZHANG (659-745)

A Note on Homecoming

I left home in an early year,
Returning now as a big, old man.
My temples show white hair,
But my home tongue, speak I can.
To me the stranger, children make a smiling inquest,
"Where did you come from, our guest?"

To Willow

A whole tree of jasper and jade is made,
With myriad green, silken cords in cascade.
Who has tailored such fine leaves?
Each early spring blast is like a scissor-blade.

CHEN ZIANG (661-702)

Climbing the Terrace of Yuzhou

Our ancestors ahead we cannot see,
Nor behind us, our posterity.
Heaven and earth long will keep.
Alone I break down and weep.

ZHANG JIULING (678-740)

Complaint, no. 2

In spring, the leaves of orchids are luxuriant.
In autumn, cassia blooms look pure and bright.
Each grows happily according to nature,
To bless a festival with its sight.

Who would know many hermits, on hearing of the flowers,
Come to sit and praise them with pleasure:
"Each herb or tree grows on its own terms.
Who would ask a beauty to clip it for her treasure?"

Complaint, no. 4

Red oranges grow in the south of Yangzi.
Their green groves through winters still thrive.
Could it be that the earth is warmer there?
In cold weather, they can, by nature, survive.

Worthy to set before our honored guests,
It is a pity they get deeply obscured.
Thus fate, very much like chance,
Goes in cycles, not to be secured.

Of planting peach and plum trees, speak they may.
This tree shades us in its own way.

Looking at the Moon and Longing for a Distant Lover

From the sea's verge, a bright moon rises
To let people from all corners share its light.
But lovers complain about the long, dark hours.
Yearnings for each other run through the night.

I love the moonbeams all over me, with my candle out,
And on my robe, feel the heavy dew.
Unable to send you a handful of the moon's radiance,
I go back to my slumber and dream about you.

WANG ZHIHUAN (688-742)

Beyond the Frontier

From the white clouds afar, the waters of the Yellow River
    flow.
Behind a lone town, to great heights the mountains go.
The Tartar pipes need not play the "Break a Willow Branch"
    tune.
Once past the Yumen Pass, there is no spring breeze or
    willow.

Climbing the Pavilion of the Storks

The white sun sinks behind the hill.
The Yellow River flows into the sea.
To eye the farthest views there may be,
Climb another floor still.

MENG HAORAN (689-740)

Drinking at the Daoist Priest Mei's Hermitage

I lie in my forest hut, sad over the end of spring,
And open my window, to view the scenery.
Suddenly I meet Blue Bird, a messenger of Qi Song.
For a visit to his house, he invites me.

The alchemist's furnace has just fired up.
Into blossoms, the magic peach tree begins to break.
If I could look forever young,
A drink of the fairy's wine I would take.

Feelings at the Beginning of Winter

Leaves fall while wild geese fly south.
Across the river, a cold, north wind has blown.
My hometown is where the Xiang River curves,
Beyond the clouds of Chu, too far to be shown.

In a land of strangers, I have shed all my homesick tears.
Watching my lone sail towards infinity,
I get lost and want to ask for help,
At dusk, on this boundless, level sea.

In the South Pavilion on a Summer Day, Thinking of Xin the Elder.

Sunlight suddenly drops behind the hill in the west.
A slow moon rises from the east above the pond in the sky.
I take in the evening cool, with my hair loosened
And by an open window, leisurely lie.

With a plash, dewdrops come off bamboos.
The breeze from the lotus carries a scent.
I want to play my lute,
But can share with none, to my lament.

For this, I long for you, old friend.
Late into the night, I dream of you without end.

Mooring at Night on the Tonglu River and Remembering an Old Friend at Guangling

I feel sad hearing the monkeys' whimper,
With a gray river rushing by in the night.
On either bank, leaves rustle in the wind.
My lone boat is well-lit by moonlight.

Jiande is not my hometown.
My old friends at Guangling are close to my heart.
Let me send my two streams of tears
To my friends, west of the river, far apart.

Mooring on the River at Jiande

By a misty isle, my moored boat is to stay.
Sunset saddens the traveler at the end of the day.
Trees in the wild get dwarfed by the vast sky.
The moon in the limpid river is nigh.

On Climbing Mount Xian with Some Friends

Human affairs, through the ages with their changes,
Link up the past and present with time.
This famous landmark of an ancient period
Remains for us to revisit and climb.

Fish traps in the shallows show at low tide.
On a cold day, the Meng marshes look deep.
Yang Hu's monument stands here still.
After reading it, I find tear-stains on my robe as I weep.

On Climbing Orchid Mountain in Autumn - a Poem for Zhang the Fifth

Amid white clouds of the North Mountain,
With joy and freedom, the hermit spends each day.
I climb this hill to see him.
On the wings of a wild goose, my heart is carried away.

Sadness rises in the dusk.
Cool autumn brings out humor at its best.
Often I see returning villagers treading on sand.
At the ferry-head, they rest.

The trees on the far horizon look tiny like caltrops.
An island by the river is shaped like the moon.
When can we come up here with wine?
To be drunk cheering mid-autumn is my boon.

On Returning to South Mountain at the Year's End

No more will I petition at the Capital.
By Mount Zhongnan, I retire to my humble home.

The wise king discards me for my inability.
I am often sick; few old friends have come.

My white hair shows and makes me look old.
Spring brings the year to a close.
I am sleepless and sad over my past.
Through the pines, a pale moon shows.

On Stopping at an Old Friend's Homestead

My old friend cooked a chicken with millet,
Inviting me to his farmhouse, and I make a call.
Green trees surround your village
While blue, sloping hills stand beyond its wall.

You open the window to show me the farm
And talk about mulberries and flax over wine to sip.
I shall wait till the Autumn Festival
To enjoy your chrysanthemums on my return trip.

Parting from Wang Wei

Quietly, what am I waiting for?
I return home empty-handed, days on end.
I want to leave for opportunities,
But hate to part with my old friend.

Who in power will help me?
In this world, those who know me are rare.
I should have stayed in solitude,
Shut by the gate of my home, from year to year.

A Poem for Minister Zhang composed by Lake Dongting

In the eighth month, the lake is level and still.
With the vast sky, its lucent immensity blends well.
But near the Yun and Meng marshes, it is a steamer,
Pounding the city wall of Yaoyang with many a swell.

I cannot cross the lake without a boat.
Untalented and idle, I feel ashamed not serving the king.
Sitting here and watching the angler cast his line,
I find envy is what my mind can bring.

Spring Dawn

Well asleep past dawn in spring,
Everywhere I hear birds sing.
In the storm last night, after the rumble,
How many flowers have been falling?

Written in the Qin Country, for a Buddhist Priest, Master Yuan

I often want to retire to a hut in the hills,
But even the funds to dig three paths, I cannot find.
Wandering in the north is not my wish.
My master at East Wood is on my mind.

Here, money burns fast like cinnamon sticks.
My ambitions wane as the years go.
Late in the day, amid a cold blast,
The cicada's chirp adds to my woe.

WANG CHANGLING (c690-756)

Complaint in the Palace of Loyalty

Near the open door of the Golden Palace,
By dawn she brooms and sweeps.
She holds a round fan at times.
Pacing back and forth, she keeps.

Compared with that of a wintry crow,
Her pretty, jade-like face is less bright.
From the Palace of Luminous Sun,
The bird can still bring back sunlight.

Going up to the Frontier

Cicadas chirp in the empty mulberry groves.
Along the Xiaoguan road, in the eighth month of the year,
Exiting one pass, we enter another,
With yellow grass and sedge everywhere.

Mercenaries from the You and Bing provinces,
For long, spent their whole lives here in battle.
Do not imitate those gallant rovers
Who praise their fast horses with many a bragging tattle.

Passing the Frontier

Under a Qin moon or through a Han pass, far away,
From expeditions, soldiers are not yet home today.
If only the "Flying General" of the Dragon City were alive,
Behind the Yin Mountains, the Tartar horsemen would
    choose to stay.

Returning from the Frontier

Crossing an autumn river and watering my horse,
I found the wind like a knife and the water cold.
The Lindao Pass, with the sun still above the level sand,
Lends a view in the darkness about to unfold.

By the Great Wall, there were battles for long.
All the soldiers then declared their spirits were high.
But yellow sands overrun this place as before,
And among heaps of weeds and thistles, white bones lie.

WANG WEI (701-761)

Autumn Night

Under a moon just rising, with slight autumn dew,
She has not changed her gauze dress, light and thin.
Into the night, in earnest, she plays her silver zither.
Fearful of an empty room, she cannot bear to go in.

Birdsong Torrent

Leisurely I watch cassia petals drop.
The spring hill is empty in the quiet night.
Moonrise gives the mountain birds a fright.
Time and again, in the vernal brook, they sing and stop

Deer Park

On an empty hill alone am I,
With just echoes of human sounds deflected.
In the deep forest, from the sky,
On green mosses shines light reflected.

Farewell

I toast you farewell, dismounted from my horse
And ask about your journey and course.
You say, "Things have not gone my way.
By Mount Zhongnan, I shall return to stay."
I ask no more, and you depart,
Like the endless white clouds, forever apart.

Farewell to Xin Jian at the Lotus Pavilion

A cold, night rain is mixed with the river as I enter Wu.
Before the lonely Chu Hill, I bid you goodbye at dawn.
My pure heart is like a piece of ice in a jade pot.
To my inquiring folks in Luoyang, give this comparison
        drawn.

Green Gully

To reach the Yellow Flower Stream,
A path along a green gully I follow,
With coils and turns by the hill,
Even on a short distance I go.

Water falls noisily among jagged rocks.
Deep in the pines, it is a calm sight,

With rippling water-chestnuts and floating hearts,
And reeds and rushes lit clear and bright.

My mind has long been leisurely,
Like this stream, so tranquil and clear.
Please allow me to stay on a big rock
And take fishing as a career.

The Hermitage of the Bamboos

I sit alone in a quiet bamboo grove,
Pluck my zither and whistle for long.
In the deep woods, unknown to men,
I am shone by a bright moon coming along.

A poem for Commissioner Li before his Departure for Zizhou

Trees shoot up to the sky from myriad ravines.
From a thousand hills, cuckoos call.
After a whole night's rain on the hills,
A hundred cascades from the treetops fall.

A tribute to you from the women there may be tong fabric,
But from the men, over taro fields, suits and rage.
Wen Weng of Han was a pioneer teacher of our culture.
You will not just rest on the groundwork by one sage.

My Retirement Villa by Mount Zhongnan

In middle age, I like Buddhist teachings
And live below Mount Zhongnan, as the years go.
In the mood, I wander there alone
And seek pleasure only I know.

Walking by a stream until it ends,
I then sit to watch the clouds on their ascent.
Talking and laughing with an old man of the woods,
I forget to go home, following my bent.

Remembrance

Red beans from the south
Sprout several shoots in spring.
I advise you to pick more.
The utmost lovesick yearnings, the beans can bring.

A Reply to Assistant Prefect Chang

In my late years I like to be quiet
And from all worldly matters free.
Since I lack a good plan for this,
Returning to my old grove may suit me.

Winds through pines loosen my girdle.
I can play the lute, under a hill, lit by the moon.
You ask about the mysteries of life.
From the far estuary, listen to the fisherman's tune.

Taking Leave of Ji Wuqian who has Failed the Official Examination and is Returning to his Village

There are no hermits in just and peaceful times.
At court, the best and the brightest all appear.
This resulted in the return of the ancient hermits.
To a life on ferns and herbs, they did not adhere.

Far you journeyed for a court post but failed,
But who would negate what you aspire.
You left home near the rivers in the Cold Food Festival.
Now at the capital, they are stitching spring attire.

Beside a road of Changan, I toast you farewell,
Seeing off a close friend to whom I can relate.
Right away you will sail in a cassia boat
And soon reach home to touch your thorn-wood gate.

By the time you arrive where the distant trees beckon,
A setting sun on this lonely city will be in view.
Even if your thoughts and plans are not put to use,
Do not say your ideas are shared by few.

Thinking of My Brothers in Shandong on the Ninth Day of the Ninth Moon

A lone guest in a strange village am I.
During each festival I doubly yearn for my family.
Afar I know my brothers are climbing high,
With dodder sprays on them, all except me.

A View of River Han

Under Mount Jingmen, near the Chu and Xiang borders,
Joining nine streams, River Han, in its flow,
Rolls on a journey beyond Heaven and Earth.
The mountain colors in the waters vaguely show.

Reflections of a village bob in the front estuary.
Among the waves, the distant sky seems to move.
On a sunny day at Xiangyang with a gentle wind,
To stay here and get drunk with a friend I would love.

Written on Returning from Mount Song

I follow a clear stream in the woods,
In my horse and carriage, feeling free.
The flowing waters seem to share my thoughts.
Homing birds at dusk return with me.

Above a deserted city facing an ancient ford,
The hills are fully bathed by sunset in the fall.
After a long descent home from Mount Song,
Let me shut my gate to all.

The Zhongnan Range

Near the capital is the Tai Yi Peak,
Linking the ranges to the seaside right through.
On turning, I find white clouds joining
And blue mists gathering to block the view.

The middle ridge divides the landscape into two scenes.
The valleys look different, shaded or bright.
I ask a woodcutter across the stream,
Wishing to find lodging from someone for the night.

LI BAI (701-762)

At a Banquet Held in Xie Tiao's Tower in Xuanzhou, to bid Farewell to Archivist Shu Yun

What left me in peace happened yesterday,
　A day that has slipped away.

What disturbs my mind comes today,
   A day that many worries stay.

Wild geese take off
On the autumn wind for many a mile.
This high tower holds a send-off.
Toasting makes the right style.

As the Archivist, your writings tell,
Of the Jian An scholars, you are a peer.
With those of Xie Tiao, they compare well,
Equally luxuriant and clear.

A flying spirit both hold,
To climb the blue sky,
And with an interest refined and bold,
Hug the bright moon on high.

Draw your sword and cut water-flow.
The flow yet will restore.
Lift your cup and drink off your woe.
Woe will grow all the more.

If in this life you feel forlorn,
With hair let loose, sail a boat next morn.

Bring in the Wine

Do you not see, from the sky, the Yellow River's waters
      come down, run to the sea and never turn back?
Do you not see, from bright mirrors, old people grieve over
      their snow-white hair that, in the morn of life, was
      silken black?
Enjoy life fully when your wishes are met.
To the moon, do not raise your empty gold goblet.
My inborn talent from Heaven will apply.

My spent wealth will return as time goes by.
Let's cook a lamb and kill an ox for our pleasure.
Let's down three hundred cups of wine in one measure.

Mister Cen and Dan Qiu, drink up.
Wine is coming for drinking from cup to cup.
I shall sing a song for you.
Please, for my sake, listen hard too.
To me, bell, drum, feast and jade are in low esteem.
Just do not wake me up from a long, drunken dream.
Ancient saints and sages we leave lonely.
Drinkers from history we know only.

At Penglai Palace, the Prince of Chen held a feast.
Over priceless wine, his guests made jests and laughs as
        pleased.
How can a host say he is short of cash?
To buy wine for my friends, I will dash.
My dappled horse is here, and behold
My furs worth a thousand in gold.
To barter these for wine, I will bid my boy go
And together drink off our age-old woe.

Chanting on the River

On the push of the magnolia oars,
My boat of spice-wood goes.
From jade flutes and gold pipes,
At two ends of the boat, music flows.

With fine wine of large volumes,
In jugs by the thousands to fill,
And women hired for company,
On the waves we drift at will.

An immortal waited for the yellow crane,
With a set plan of action.
A seafarer like me, with no chart in mind,
Follows the white gull for direction.

Quyuan's verses earn high respect.
Among the sun and the moon, they stand.
But the terraces and pavilions of King Chu
Have become barren, hilly land.

In high spirits, I pen a piece
That can shake the five peaks above.
My finished poem makes me smile
And pride over those in the hermits' cove.

If lasting glory and riches can be found,
River Han would be northwest bound.

Drinking alone under the Moon

Amid flowers with a pot of wine,
I drink alone with none that I know.
Raising my cup to invite the bright moon,
I have a party of three with my shadow.

The moon understands nothing of drinking.
My shadow is a mere follower of me.
For now they are my companions.
Before spring leaves, let us be merry.

I sing - the moon lingers.
I dance - my shadow is in disarray.
Awake, we shall have fun together.
Drunk, each on his own gets away.

Forever bonded and fully engaged in play,
I hope for a reunion on the Milky Way some day.

Farewell to Meng Haoran for Guangling

From the Yellow Crane Tower, my old friend goes
West to Yangzhou, amid mist and flower early spring
   shows.
Afar your lone sail becomes a shadow, at the blue sky's end.
As I watch on, to Heaven's verge, only the Yangzi flows.

For Meng Haoran

Master Meng is the one I love.
His grace and style, people well know and admire.
He scorned rank and wealth when young.
White-haired, he lies under pine and cloud to retire.

Often drunk under moonlight like the lofty ancients,
He is attached to flowers, not kings for a post to secure.
Who can reach a high mountain of a man like you?
Vainly I try to copy your character, fragrant and pure.

Going down to Jiangling

At dawn I leave Baidi amid clouds in a colorful array
And reach faraway Jiangling in a day.
On either shore is the endless chatter of the gibbons.
Past myriad hills, my light boat has glided away.

The Moon

When I was not taught and very small,
I called the moon a white jade plate with a sheen,
Or a flying mirror from the fairy's terrace,
Edging clouds, jasper-like and bluish-green.

The Moon at the Border

Emerging from Tian Shan, a bright moon moves,
Among vast layers of clouds, on its way.
A wind sweeps over the Yumen Pass,
After coming from myriad miles away.

At the Baidengdao Hill, Liu Bang of Han escaped.
Lake Kokonor is still under the Tartars' surveillance.
This has been a key battleground for years.
To return home, none had a chance.

When soldiers guard and view the desolate frontiers,
Their homesick looks show bitterness and pain.
I believe in a high tower tonight,
Their loved ones must be sighing again and again.

Night Thoughts

Before my bed, bright moonlight is found,
Taken for the glare of a frosty ground.
I raise my head to watch the bright moon
And bow to think of my hometown.

On Climbing Phoenix Tower at Jinling

The vacant Phoenix Terrace was a haunt of the phoenix.
Now just the Yangzi flows on.
Buried along secluded paths, the blooms of the Wu Palace
    lie.
Into ancient burial mounds, the nobles of Jin have gone.

The Three Peaks get half-sunk in the blue sky beyond.
From the white Egret Isle, into two the river is torn.

Since floating clouds always block the sun,
Losing sight of Changan makes me forlorn.

On the Mountain: a Conversation

You ask me why I live on Jade Mountain.
I smile and keep quiet, with a carefree mind.
With peach flowers on water flowing freely by,
It is a different world, not for mankind.

Pining

Drawing her pearl blind, a pretty woman sits.
For long, her moth-like brows she knits.
Wet traces of weeping show,
But I do not know who gave her woe.

Resolutions after being Drunk on a Spring Day

Spend your time on earth, like in a big dream.
Why toil the whole life until you die?
So it is that I can drink all day.
In the front porch, slovenly I lie.

Awake, I look across the yard
And hear a bird among the flowers sing.
Pray tell me what day this is.
I talk to an oriole, amid the winds of spring.

At this, with a thoughtful mind, I sigh,
Pour wine for myself again,
And sing loudly and grandly, in wait for the moon.
After singing, my highest spirits I attain.

Sending off a friend to the Kingdom of Shu

They say the road to the Kingdom of Shu
Is too rugged to travel, even worse.
Mountains rise from the rider's face.
Clouds emerge by the head of his horse.

Scented trees wrap the plank-paths of Qin.
Winding the city-wall are streams in spring.
Your ups and downs in life are parts of fate.
There is no need to ask the diviner for anything.

Toast with a Hermit

Amid blooms in the hill, both you and I
Empty one cup, get drunk and then I say,
"I want to sleep; leaving me, you should try,
But if willing, return with a flute the next day."

Lady Yang

I

Her cloud-like dress, flower-like face
And dense dews on petals, gentle spring winds embrace.
If she is not seen on the hills of Fairyland,
Meet her under the moon on the Immortals' Jade Terrace.

II

A red, pretty peony with distilled, scented dew.
We grieve over the story at Wu Hill, sad but untrue.
Who in the Han Palace could look like her?
The lovely Lady Flying Swallow, when adorned anew.

On a famed flower and empire-wrecker, in mutual delight,
The King often beams and fixes his sight.
To explain the endless jealousy of the spring wind,
North of the Hidden Fragrance Pavilion, they lean on the
    railing, day until night.

Viewing the Waterfall of Mount Lu

Like a censer, the sunlit peak lets a purple haze free.
The waterfall hanging like a long stream, from afar we see.
Flying straight down for three thousand feet,
The Milky Way of High Heavens, it is thought to be.

A Visit to a Priest

A dog's bark comes through the noisy, running stream.
Peach flowers in the rain make a lush display.
At times I see a deer in the deep grove.
Near the creek, I hear not the bell by midday.

Wild bamboos share the green mists.
From the jade-like peak, waterfalls rapidly drop down.
None knows where the priest has gone.
So, leaning on some pine branches, I frown.

DU FU (712-770)

Climbing on the Double Ninth Day

Birds circle above the limpid water of the white sandbar.
In the strong wind of the tall sky, gibbons sadly cry.

Leaves come rustling down in the boundless forest.
The endless Yangzi comes rolling by.

I am sad in autumn, often miles away as a traveler.
Sick my whole life, I climb the terrace alone.
Hardships and bitter regrets whiten my hair.
Down and out, away with my wine cup I have just done.

Dreaming of Li Bai

I

To bid farewell to the dead,
I swallow my sobs and lower my head.
For a friend living apart,
Constant woe is in my heart.

To a land of miasma you have gone,
South of the Yangzi alone.
But you, as a guest in exile,
Have no news for a long while.

In a dream you came to me,
Knowing your long presence in my memory.
You are now trapped in a net.
The wings to fly here, how did you get?

You arrive not as a living soul, I fear,
For you are immeasurably far from here.
When your soul comes, maples are seen,
All alive and turning green.

Your soul will leave and go back
To passes and hills, dark and black.

Moonlight falls fully upon the beam.
Your lit face shows, it would seem.

The water around you is quite deep.
Fighting the broad waves, you have to keep.
I pray you would have the chance to win
And not let a flood dragon pull you in.

II

All day long, floating clouds move on.
The wanderer returns not, though long gone.
For three nights in my dream, you came to me,
Showing regards, warm and friendly.

Your departure is always rushed with no delay.
"Coming here is not easy," you bitterly say,
"Disputes are often in the voyage of life.
My boat may sink in the strife."

You leave, scratching your white hair.
Burdening life-ambitions, you seem to bear.
All over the capital, many officials excel and glow.
You alone are feeling depressed and low.

Who says Heaven's net of justice is wide?
Getting old, from injustice you cannot hide.
For ten thousand years, a man's fame cannot last.
The dead is always forgotten and bypassed.

Gazing at the Great Mount

Mount Dai, what splendid wonder!
How to pen my thoughts, I ponder.
Green valleys and hills extend

For miles without end.
The Maker's mystic beauty, cut in light or shade,
At dawn or dusk, has been made.
My mind gets stirred as clouds in layers rise.
At homing birds, I strain my eyes.
I shall conquer the very peak and see
How small other hills will be.

Moonlit Night

Tonight this moon in Fuzhou
Alone my wife stays up to see.
My tender thoughts rest with my children,
Too young to remember Changan and me.

Your cloud-like hair must be wet with mist;
Your jade-like arm chilled under the clear moonlight.
When can we lean by the curtain and look up together?
Dry-eyed, we shall be out of this plight.

New Moon

Not yet in its first quarter,
The new moon sheds weak light.
The slender, slanting moonbeams
Form an arc that is not yet tight.

Beyond an old fortress,
It barely rises in the sky,
And already stays covered
At the edge of dusk clouds nearby.

The Milky Way up above
Changes not its luster bold.
The passes and the hills

On their own have turned cold.

In my front courtyard,
There is colorless dew.
In the dark, to the full,
It soaks the chrysanthemums through.

On Leaving Marshall Fang's Tomb

Between stops on my trip in a strange land,
I stay my horse to bid your lone grave goodbye.
Approaching while weeping, I wet the soil with my tears.
Broken bits of clouds hang low in the sky.

Wish I had the chance to play chess with Grand Tutor Xie
Or a fine sword for the Lord of Xu to bring.
But I see only fallen petals in the grove
And hear, for this guest, farewell chants that orioles sing.

Spring Prospect

Hills and rivers remain, but the kingdom is done.
In spring, by deep grasses and trees, the city is overrun.
I feel the change; flowers in view set my tears free.
I am sad on leaving; crying birds startle me.
The steady beacon fires are three months old.
A letter from home takes ten thousand in gold.
My scratched white hair, getting short and thin,
Cannot really hold a hatpin.

Thinking of My Brothers on a Night of Moonlight

The region is deserted, save the beat of war-drums

And the cry of an autumn wild goose at the frontier.
White dews will start from tonight.
In my old village, the moon must be bright and clear.

The brothers I have are all scattered.
There is none at home to ask if they are alive.
My letters have never got there for long.
Besides, the enlisted soldiers are still in strife.

The Visitor

South and north of my hut runs spring water.
Every day I see flocks of gulls come through.
The path with flowers has not been swept for guests.
The bramble gate is now first open for you.

Far from the market, my dishes are few.
I am poor; my old wine is a scoff.
Will you drink with this old man from next door?
I shall shout over the hedge and let's finish it off.

WANG HAN (fl. 713)

The Song of Liangzhou

Such fine grape-wine in a night-glowing cup so rare!
But a "Hurry to Horseback" tune, the pipa does blare.
If I should lie drunk on the battlefield, do not laugh.
For long, how many soldiers return from warfare?

CEN SHEN (715-770)

Climbing the Pagoda at Zien Monastery with Gao Shi and Xue Chu

The pagoda seems to burst from the earth,
Soaring to the Heavenly Palaces alone.
We leave the world by climbing
And circling the void on steps of stone.

Abrupt and steep, it dominates this blessed land.
Harsh and sharp, the work of Spirits it is well nigh.
Its four corners block the white sun.
Its seven stories touch the gray sky.

Peering down to point at flying birds
And leaning over to hear the wind's alarming sound,
We see waves in the ranges,
Running together as if eastward bound.

I find green locust trees lining the imperial highway,
And palaces and pavilions in intricate style.
Autumn colors will come from the west,
To overshadow Guanzhong grimly for many a mile.

The fine imperial tombs up in the north plains
For millenia have stayed drizzly and green.
I can comprehend the Theory of Purity.
For long, a believer of "Cause and Effect" I have been.

I vow in my office I shall not remain.
To be enlightened in the Way is endless gain.

On Meeting a Messenger Going to the Capital

My sleeves fail to keep my teary eyes dry
As I look east to my old home far away.
Encountering you on horseback with no brush or paper,
A message that I am safe, please relay.

GAO SHI (716-765)

Seeing off Assistant-Magistrate Li Degraded to Xiazhong and Assistant-Magistrate Wang degraded to Changsha

Alas! Gentlemen, how do you feel on leaving like this?
As I ask about your exile, stay your horse and drink.
At Wu Gorge, the monkeys' screeching will make you weep.
From Hengyang, how many letters can the returning wild
geese bring?

Autumn sails go far on the Green Maple River.
Near the White Emperor City, few old trees have survived
and stood.
The king's favor drips like dew and rain in this great era.
Over this brief parting, you need not brood.

ZU YONG (early 8th century)

Looking at the Snow Drifts on South Mountain

South of the mountain, the view is fair,
With floating clouds fringing its drifts of snow.

The clear, sunlit sky trims the woods with a glow.
At night, in the city, it is much colder to bear.

LI QI (fl. 725)

An Old Theme

A soldier fighting afar is what a man should be,
Modeling after the warriors of Yu and Yen since childhood.
They fought for mastery under trampling horses
And held their lives light but principles good.
None dared approach them after a killing.
Like porcupine quills, their beards stood

Through flying, white dust-clouds under the mound's yellow
      sandstorms,
They could not go home till the king's favors were repaid.
Adept at pipa, dancing and singing,
From Liao Dong, a fifteen-year-old maid,
On her Tartar flute, piped a "Leaving the Frontier" tune.
Raining down their cheeks, the soldiers' tears were made.

On Seeing Wei Wan off to the Capital

I hear travelers sing the song of farewell at daybreak.
Last night, the Yellow River had its first frost-spray.
I cannot bear hearing the wild geese, in my sadness,
While into the clouded hills, my friend is just on his way.

I see the glow of dawn and feel the chill in the frontier city.
By dusk, the noise of the washerwomen's pounding I hear.
Changan is no longer a city for pleasure.
Time is easily wasted if your goal is not clear.

LU LUN (c748-c798)

Farewell to Li Duan

My old home is rank with weeds.
Leaving you for home, I feel sad and low,
To be on a road beyond the cold clouds
And arrive in the evening snow.

Early orphaned, I wandered as a young man
And came to know you late, after many disasters at hand.
We face each other speechless, covering our tears.
Through winds and dust, when shall we meet in this land?

HAN HONG (mid 8th century)

Festival of Cold Food

Petals fly all over the city in spring.
On Cold Food Day, the east wind bends the royal willows.
By dusk, the Han palace bestows candles
On the Five Dukes, whose light smoke shows.

A Reply to Cheng Jin's Poem, written in the Same Measure

Long bamboo stems face the morning wind.
The empty city is quiet under moonlight.
A wild goose in autumn crosses the Milky Way.
Mallots on myriad washing-stones sound at night.

It is late autumn, as the season goes.
I put off sleep, with my mind on your meeting me.
Always an admirer of your elegant lines,
As the morning crows caw, I still work on my poetry.

JI WUQIAN (early 8th century)

Spring Boating on Reye Stream

In quietude undisturbed,
I float on a stream, carried in by chance,
In a boat blown by a twilight wind,
With flower banks all the way to the entrance.

By night I turn to the west creek,
To view, beyond the hills, the Southern Dipper above.
Over the pool, massive mists fly,
With the moon hanging low behind a grove.

The cares of life are boundless and beyond our control.
Wish I could be an old man with a fishing pole.

LIU ZHANGQING (c719-c787)

Climbing to the Monastery on General Wu's Terrace and Surveying the Prospect on an Autumn Day

At this deserted, ancient terrace,
In autumn I arrive with a homesick heart.
The temple in the wild draws few visitors.
By a deep stream and high mountain, it is set apart.

Sunset rests on some old ramparts.
A cold bell fills the empty grove with its chime.
I am depressed over the Southern Dynasties.
Only the flowing Yangzi is the survivor of time.

Farewell to the Monk Ling Che

From the Bamboo Grove Monastery, amid the greenery,
Comes the chime of the evening bell, far away.
Alone, on your return to the distant, green hills,
Your bamboo hat carries slanting sunbeams of the day.

Looking for Chang, the Daoist Recluse of South Stream

I leave footprints on the green moss
All along the road that I pass.
White clouds hang over a quiet sandbar.
Idle doors stay shut behind spring grass.

After a rain, I enjoy the beauty of pine trees
And follow a stream to its source on the hill.
In the presence of flowers and spirituality,
What is more to say still?

The Lute Player

I hear the cold notes of "Pine Wind" in silence.
Empowering are the sounds of your seven-string lute.
I myself love ancient music
Which most contemporaries refute.

On Seeing Wang the Eleventh Leave for the South

The vast mists and waters will separate us
As I wave you goodbye here in tears.
Where did the birds fly off?
Like a vacant mass, the green hill appears.

Your lone sail flows on the Yangzi far away.
In spring, the five lakes light up at sunset.
Who would see me on this river strand of white duckweeds,
And feel the parting woe that I get?

Written at New Year

My homesick thoughts are keen by the New Year.
Alone at the sky's verge, I am in tears.
An old man like me still works for others.
Before my homebound trip, another spring appears.

Mountain monkeys share my days and nights,
By riverside willows, in a mist or blast.
I am like the imperial tutor banished to Changsha.
How many more years will my exile last?

YUAN JIE (719-772)

Addressed to my Officials and Subordinates after the Retreat of the Rebels

At former, more peaceful times,
I lived among hills and trees for two decades.
A spring bubbled up from my courtyard,
And caves were found before my gates.

48

At set periods, they collected taxes.
Until the sun was late, a tight sleep one could deserve.
Suddenly I met, in this area, unrest and change.
For years, under war banners, I had to serve.

Now that I am here to govern this county,
Mountain bandits are disbanded and gone.
They do not care now to ransack this little town.
Pitifully, our people are poor after the hurt is done.

Thus the neighboring region is under ravage,
Only leaving this district unmolested.
Those envoys with a mandate from the emperor -
Are they any different from the thieves that infested?

Those tax collectors oppressed the commoners,
Like frying them on fire.
Who would take people's lives
And still be called this world's squire?

I wish to give up my official duties.
Pushing my boat off with a stake,
I would reside where fish and millet grow,
And get old by a lake.

DAI SHULUN (732-789)

On Meeting at an Inn an Old Friend from my Village in Jiangnan

A full moon shines again in autumn,
On the city wall, with the thick, dark sky behind.
Our reunion south of the Yangzi
Is dream-like and a re-doubt in my mind.

A wind startles the magpies on the dark branches.
The sound of cold crickets, wet grasses quell.
We travelers drink for long over our togetherness;
Parting again is right at the dreaded, morning bell.

WEI YINGWU (737-c792)

Anchoring at Yu Yi in the Evening

As my sail gets lowered to stop at a town of River Huai,
I moor the boat near a lone courier stop.
A strong wind beats up the waves
While below the horizon, the dusk sun is to drop.

People return as the hills and village walls darken.
On islets lit with reeds, wild geese land to rest.
I find myself alone, thinking of my home at Qin Pass
And listening to the temple bell, as a sleepless guest.

A Farewell to Li Cao in the Rain

It is drizzling on the Yangzi
When the evening bells of Nanjing go.
The sails come in quietly and look heavy.
Taking off in the dark, birds fly slow.

Trees on the far shore look damp.
Lost afar is the opening to the sea.
My parting woe is boundless.
Like loose silk, tears wet my robe and run free.

A Ferry West of Chuzhou

I care only for hidden grasses by the stream.
Deep in the trees above, yellow orioles chant.
With the evening rain, rapid spring tides team.
At the deserted ferry, empty boats lie aslant.

A Lucky Meeting on the River Huai with an Old Friend from Liangzhou

I once traveled on the Han and Yangzi,
Returning drunk after each meeting with you.
Since then, we have drifted away like floating clouds.
Ten years, as water flows, have slipped through.

Our joy and friendship are the same as old.
Our hair has gone thinner and grayer still.
Why do you have to return to the north,
Leaving me on River Huai, facing the autumn hill?

On the Eastern Outskirts

Cramped in my office all year long,
I go to the outskirts, at the break of day.
Willows sway in the breeze.
Blue hills clear my cares away.

I rest at ease by a tree
And walk along a green stream, time and again.
Where comes a spring pigeon's song?
A drizzle moistens the fragrant plain.

My wish to seek a retreat is often blocked.
Office and personal routines irritate me.

At the end, I shall quit and build a hut here.
Like my admired Tao Qian, I would almost be.

LIU SHENXU (fl.742-755)

Poem

This road ends with white clouds.
The clear brook, in a long stretch like a spring day,
Carries fallen petals from time to time
And their scent on the flow far away.

My study fronts the hilly road,
In the shade of willows, buried deep.
The branches and leaves cover me, now and then.
But lighting up my robe, sunshine can keep.

CUI SHU (d.739)

Climbing Wang Xian Terrace on the Double Ninth: Presented to Vice-Prefect Liu

Emperor Wen of Han built a high terrace.
Today I climb it at the break of dawn.
Clouds and hills on the Three Jins lie to the north.
To the Two Tombs, wind and rain from the east are drawn.

The guardian of the frontier gate is now known by none.
The immortal of the river stayed away, once departed.
I would rather be searching around here for Peng Ze,

On chrysanthemum wine, both to be fuddled and light-
hearted.

CUI HAO (d.754)

Passing Hua Yin

Overlooking Xian Yang are the lofty Hua Mountains.
None can chisel and shape the three peaks beyond the skies.
Clouds are parting before the temple of Emperor Wu.
The first sun shows on the Fairy's Palm Hill as rain dries.

Mountains and rivers lie north of the perilous Qin Pass.
West to the Han temple on the plain, courier roads head.
Let me ask the wayside seekers of fortune and fame,
If they would rather study immortality here instead.

Yellow Crane Pavilion

On a yellow crane, an ancient immortal flew away.
Just an empty Yellow Crane Pavilion is left here.
Once gone, the yellow crane never comes back.
For myriad years, in the boundless sky, only white clouds
        appear.

You can see clearly sun-lit streams among the trees of Han
        Yang.
On Parrot Isle, fragrant grasses thrive.
But, in the sunset, where is my old village?
At the river's wave and mist, my sad feelings revive.

ZHANG JI (mid 8th century)

Anchored at Night by Maple Bridge

Crows caw at a moonless, all-frosty sky.
Facing river maples and the fisherman's torch, I sadly lie.
Beyond the city of Suzhou, the Cold Mountain Temple bell
Chimes at midnight, reaching passenger-boats that ply.

LIU YUXI (772-842)

Black Gown Lane

By Red Bird Bridge, weeds show their florets.
On Black Gown Lane, slanting rays fall as the sun sets.
The swallows that nested in the Wang and Xie mansions
Have flown to the commoners' hamlets.

Song of Bamboo Twigs

By a calm river, green willows grow.
Into my ears, on the river, his songs flow.
Sunrise is in the east, rain in the west.
They say it is sunless, but to me sunbeams show.

A Spring Song

From the red pavilion, a newly adorned lady steps down.
A spring scene behind locked gates is the cause of her frown.
She walks to the courtyard and counts the flowers.

Only a dragonfly flies up to her jade hairpin by the crown.

BAI JUYI (772-842)

Song of Lasting Regret

I

Bent on female charm that could wreck an empire,
The Han King sought his beauty for years in vain.
From the home of Yang, a daughter just matured.
Sheltered and unknown, she was raised to remain.

Of inborn beauty and hard to be left alone,
One day she was picked to serve the king by his arm.
When she turned and flashed an enticing smile,
All other palace ladies lost their charm.

In the Huaqing Pool, one cold, spring day,
The warm, soft water cleansed her white body in the bare.
On the maid's arm, she rose, faint and weak.
The King began to favor her in their love affair.

A golden headdress topped the cloud-like hair on her
          blooming face.
Many spring nights with the King in a warm bed she shared.
Spring nights went fast with the sun climbing high.
Henceforth, for morning court audiences, the King never
          cared.

She got busy attending to the King's feasts and pleasure.
On spring days and nights, it was the same.
Three thousand pretty ladies in the palace
Were no match for this favorite dame.

In a gilded mansion, she met his needs at night.
In a jade tower, all feasted and drunk they got.
Fife and rank were bestowed to all her siblings.
Tender glory on her household she ably sought.

Thus all parents in the nation took this to heart.
They now preferred boys less than baby girls fair.
Into the clouds, the tall palace seemed to merge.
Heard all over, heavenly music floated everywhere.

In soft beats, she made slow songs and dance steps.
The King did not have enough at the end of the day.
From You Yang, war drumbeats rocked the ground.
The song and dance broke up; the shock did stay.

II

From the city walls, smoke and dust surged.
The King's retreating cavalries headed southwest.
Her rattling journey in a carriage started and stopped,
West of the capital, about a hundred miles at best.

The armies would not march - what could be done?
To die before the horsemen, the weak, pliant lady was made.
Her headdress fell to the ground, picked up by none:
Kingfisher feathers, golden birds and combs of jade.

Unable to save her, the King covered his face.
With blood in his tears, he turned back to look.
Yellow dust scattered in the cold, silent wind,
En route to the Sword Pavilion, on hilly paths he took.

Below Mount Emei, travelers were few.
In the dim sunlight, the King's standards looked dull.
By the green hills and rivers in Sichuan,
Day after day, night after night, he was mournful.

Sighting the moon in his traveling palace broke his heart.
The sound of bells in the night rain made his guts tear.
With the earth-shaking unrest settled, the King's cavalries
        returned.
But to leave the fatal spot, he could not bear.

Below the slope of Mount Mawei, at death she lay.
But now her jade-like face was not to be found.
The King and his men all looked at each other and wept.
Then east to the capital on horseback, they turned around.

III

On return, the garden and pools stayed the same:
Taiyi Lake, Weiyang Palace, water-lilies, willows and
        all.
Water-lilies looked like her face; willow leaves her brows.
Reminded of her, the King's tears could not but fall.

There were spring windy days with peach and pear blooms.
Then came rainy autumns when wutong leaves dropped.
Now south of the Western Palace, fall weeds grew rank.
From palace steps, the sweeping of red foliage stopped.

The court actors and musicians had new, white hair.
Older than before, the eunuchs and maids did grow.
He mused in silence while fireflies hovered in the night
        palace.
Sleep would not come though the wick of his only lamp
        burned low.

Through long nights, for each slow watch to wait,
At the Milky Way, in the pre-dawn hours, he did stare.
Roof tiles with carved mandarin ducks were cold with heavy
        frost.
His feathered quilt was chilled, with none to share.

IV

Now the living was separated from the dead for a year.
In his dream, her spirit did not come still.
From Linqiong, a Daoist priest, who traveled to the capital,
Claimed he could draw her soul with dedication and skill.

Moved by the King's restless yearnings,
They had the priest make a thorough quest.
He flew like lightning through clouds in the sky,
Then deep under the earth everywhere, without rest.

He searched the Blue Sky above and the Yellow Spring
          below,
In two boundless spaces, without catching her sight.
Then he heard a mystic mountain had risen from the sea,
Standing amid a blurry, airy void in its light.

Into the clouds, delicate towers and chambers soared.
There lived many fairies, poised and full of grace.
One called Tai Zhen almost resembled her,
With her snow-white skin and flower-like face.

V

He smote the jade bolt for the West Chamber behind a
          golden gate.
And asked the maids to have his mission relayed.
She woke from a dream, upon hearing of the King's envoy.
Within the nine-flowered bed-curtain, she felt afraid.

She was up, grabbing a dress and pushing her pillow aside,
Hesitant at first to pass the open pearl curtain and silver
          screen-wall.
Though her cloud-like hair was half crumpled from sleep,
With her floral crown off, she stepped down into the hall.

58

The fairy sleeves fluttered, caught by the wind
As if in a "Rainbow Skirt and Feathered Coat" dance
        display.
Tears from her lonely, lovely face dripped onto the railing,
Like a spray of pear flowers on a rainy, spring day.

She thanked the King with a heart-felt stare.
The chance of sighting and hearing each other became small.
In the Zhaoyang Hall, their love came to an end.
In the Palace of Penglai, time seemed to stall.

Turning to scan the human world below,
She saw no capital city, but dust and fog from above.
She sent back two old objects from the King:
A case for filigrees and a gold hairpin, as his pledge of love.

One half of the case and hairpin she kept,
Splitting the gold and the filigree.
"Only if the King's mind were firm as gold," she said,
"Somewhere in Heaven or on earth, each other we would
        see."

On leaving, she repeated their old pledge in earnest,
With a vow that only both she and the King knew,
Made in the Changsheng Hall, on the seventh day of the
        seventh moon,
Alone at midnight, whispered by the two.

"In Heaven, as birds we shall fly with our wings aligned.
On earth as trees, we stay with branches entwining fast."
Heaven and earth at one point may end,
But their endless regret will last.

LIU ZONGYUAN (773-819)

Living by a Brook

Long restrained by official hat and garb,
In exile to the southern wilds, I was luckily sent.
Leisurely I live near farmers' plots.
The chance to be a hermit, I am lent.

The dewy grass is turned over at dawn.
At dusk, oars hitting pebbles give a ring.
I move about without meeting anyone.
To the blue sky of Chu, for long I sing.

Morning Walk in Autumn

Amid heavy frost and dew at autumn's end,
In a secluded valley, I walk one early morn.
Yellow leaves cover the stream and bridge.
Only old trees stand in the village, deserted and worn.

Sparse flowers in the cold are lonely.
Now and then, the secluded spring's whimper I hear.
My scheming mind has long been lost.
What is it that startles a young deer?

River Snow

Over a thousand hills, all birds fly off and go.
On myriad paths, human footprints fail to show.
A man in a bamboo cape and hat
Fishes from a lone boat in the cold river of snow.

YUAN ZHEN (779-831)

Elegy, no. 1

At home you got the most attention and love,
Like the Xue's youngest daughter in times of old.
When you married me, like poor Qian Lou,
You met setbacks a hundred fold.

Seeing that I needed clothes,
Your yellow baskets you ransacked.
Pushing me to buy wine,
You pawned your gold hairpin, for the funds I lacked.

Wild plants served as your food.
Long bean leaves you gladly tried.
Fallen leaves became your fuel.
On an old locust tree, you relied.

Now that I have a salary
Of ten thousand in excess.
With a vegetable dish to honor your death,
An elegy before your altar I address.

Elegy, no. 2

In the past, about after-life, I used to joke.
Now, before my eyes, at death I look.
I have nearly given away your clothes, but put on hold
All your embroidery that I did not bear to unfold.

I recall your kindness to the servants and devotion to me.
After you came into my dreams, I burnt you paper money.
None is spared this grief, I truly know.
For a poor couple like us, we had a hundred bundles of woe.

Elegy, no. 3

I grieve for you and myself
When I can freely sit down.
A century is a long while,
But how much time for us can be found.

Deng You lost a son.
He accepted what fate is meant to be.
Pan Yue lost his wife,
On whom he heaped poetry.

In the deep earth quite unseen,
What hope can I keep for a common grave?
In the other life, more unsure,
What chance for a reunion can I have?

I can only open my eyes
And through the nights, think of my wife.
You have unsmilingly worked all those days with me.
I want to repay you for putting up with strife.

JIA DAO (779-843)

The Absent Hermit

Under a pine tree, to my query, the child replied,
"Collecting herbs, my master has gone,
Into an unknown spot where the mists are wide.
Only this hill is where he hiked on"

LI SHEN (780-846)

"Old Style"

From one grain in springtime sown,
For the fall harvest, myriad grains are grown.
There are no idle fields under the sky.
Yet of hunger, farmers die.

They hoe rice fields right at noon.
Sweat drips to the soil just as soon.
At a meal, who would know the pain
Of planting and harvesting each grain?

CUI HU (c796)

At a Homestead South of the Capital

At this door today, in the past year,
Both your face and peach flowers lit up, pink and fair.
Now peach flowers still beam on in the spring wind,
But your face is gone and who knows where.

LI SHE (fl.806)

Half-day Leisure in the Hills

All day I get sleepy with a drunken dream,
Then struggle to go uphill, hearing spring is going away.

In the courtyard with bamboos, I talk to a monk,
Again slacking off, in my fleeting life, for half a day.

ZHU QINGYU (early 9th century)

The Approaching Examination: for Zhang Ji

Last night in the bridal chamber,
Red candles stood.
At dawn, in the hall, she pays respect
To her in-laws as a new bride should.

After washing and dressing,
She asks her husband in a low tone,
"To the current style of brows,
In the right shade are mine done?"

Within the Palace

Quiet and still is this flowering season,
In a garden shut off by the palace gate.
Shoulder to shoulder, on a grand, long corridor,
Court ladies stand and wait.

With much on their minds about the Inner Palace,
Each other they want to tell.
But face to face with the parrot,
On these gossips they dare not dwell.

LI YI (late 8th-early 9thcenturies)

Joy at Meeting a Cousin and saying Farewell again

Ten years of unrest and separation are over.
I meet you again and you have grown tall.
First I ask your family, feeling startled.
Then you say your name, and your young face I recall.

We talk of life and its changes since parted
Until the chime of the evening bell.
Tomorrow when you leave on the Baling Road,
How many autumn hills will block us, who can tell?

Marching to Shouxiang at Night and Hearing a Pipe

Before reaching the Huilou Peak, the desert is like snow.
Beyond the Shouxiang city shines frost-like moonlight.
Somewhere, someone blows a reed pipe.
All soldiers are homesick through the night.

LIU FANGPING (8th-9th centuries)

Spring Bitterness

Sunset through her window gauze is followed by twilight.
In her empty chamber, tear drops mark her face.
Spring is off its prime in the vacant, lonely courtyard,
Shut off with fallen pear flowers all over the place.

LIU ZHONGYONG (8th-9th centuries)

A Soldier's Complaint

Either at the Jin river or the Yumen Pass,
Year after year, I am a conscript.
A horse-whip and a sword hilt,
Day after day, my hands gripped.

The green graves of the frontier
Get covered in spring by white snow.
The Yellow River for myriad miles,
Around the Black Mountain, does flow.

ZHANG HU (9th century)

Jiling Terrace, no. 1

On Jiling Terrace, when slanting sunbeams appear,
Dawn mists around red-flowered trees begin to clear.
Last night, with a roster, the King entitled his new beauty.
A smiling Lady Yang, through the blinds, is to enter here.

Jiling Terrace, no. 2

The favor of the King's audience is to be borne.
The Duchess enters the palace on horseback by morn.
She has slightly touched-up brows and an unpainted face.
Rouge and powder on her fair skin is scorn.

To a Court Lady

Behind the palace gates, moonlight passes over a tree.
Two nesting egrets, her wistful eyes only see.
By the lamp, she bends and pulls out her jade hair-pin,
To tear apart the red flame and set a moth free.

Written on the Wall of Jinling Ferry-House

At Jinling Ferry-Head, in a hut on a small mound,
In woe, the overnight traveler can well be found.
Slanting moonbeams shine on the night ebb-tide.
Where the few flickers show, Guazhou must be around.

DU QIUNIANG (early 9th century)

The Coat with the Gold Threads

Cherish not your gold-threaded coat, in warning I say,
But rather the time of each youthful day.
Pluck a flower right at its prime.
Do not wait for a bare, twiggy spray.

DU MU (803-852)

Autumn Night

With her silver candle by a cold painted screen, in the lit
    autumn night,

She flaps at fireflies with a gauze fan, small and light.
Sitting by open-air steps, in the evening, cool like water,
Of the Cowherd and Weavermaid stars, she takes in the
    sight.

Confession

South of the Yangzi, as a dejected wino I stay.
Many games of love with slim southern beauties I play.
From the brothels of Yangzhou, a ten-year dream I have won
And the label "The Heartless Client in his Day".

Given in Farewell, no. 1

A thirteen-year-old girl, so slender.
A nutmeg bud of the second moon, so tender.
In the spring breeze, for miles on Yangzhou Road,
She beats all courtesans in her splendor.

Given in Farewell, no. 2

She is amorous, yet seems callous in the main.
Just a smile over our farewell drink she cannot feign.
Only the caring candle shares our parting woe,
Shedding until dawn its tears of pain.

Climbing Loyou Hill before Leaving for Wuxing

In peaceful times, I like to serve but lack the skill.
I like clouds and quiet monks, being idle and still.
Now that I shall be a magistrate beyond the waters,
Let me first view Daizhong's tomb on Loyou Hill.

Climbing Mount Qi on the Ninth Day of the Ninth Moon

The river mirrors the full fall scene, with the first migrant
    wild geese.
My friends and I take a wine pot and climb a green hill.
Hard it is on earth for one to laugh out loud.
So, on return, chrysanthemums all on my head I should fill.

To celebrate the festival, let us get drunk.
Why should we lament over sunset after climbing high.
This is the only known way since the old days.
The Bull Hill is not just a place to cry.

For Assistant Prefect Han Chuo of Yangzhou

The far, blue hills darken where the waters still carry.
Grasses have not died by fall's end, south of the Yangzi.
On the bridge named after twenty-four pretty flutists,
In the moonlit night, where do you coach your lady?

Mooring on the Qinhuai River

The sands of a cold, misty river are moonlit bright.
I moor my boat near a wine-shop for the night.
The songstress knows not the grief of a lost kingdom.
Across the river, her song is still sensual and light.

For the Wu Jiang Pavilion

Victory or defeat in war defies prediction.
A man can also accept shame and lie low.
Able and gallant are the young men east of the Yangzi.
Soon you may return on a fast horse - who would know?

The Red Cliff

A broken lance has been buried in sand.
Untarnished, its metal goes.
After my washing and rubbing,
The mark of a former dynasty shows.

If Zhou Yu in battle was not helped,
By the advantage that the east wind could bring,
The two Qiao beauties would be locked
In the Bronze Bird Pavilion, in the prime of spring.

WEN TINGYUN (812-870)

Complaint of a Jade Lute

Dreamless and sleepless in a silvery-white bed,
On a cool bamboo mat I lie.
The evening clouds are light,
Against a jade-like, water-clear sky.

Towards the Xiao and Xiang Rivers,
Far the cry of the wild geese goes.
Among tall buildings of the capital,
Alone a bright moon shows.

Ferrying South at Lizhou

The limpid water clearly reflects slanting sunbeams.
Lost in the mountain mists, crooked islets vaguely show.
The ferry has left on the waves as horses neigh.
Waiting for the ferry's return, men rest by a willow.

Gulls scatter among a few clumps of dune-grass.
Across many paddy-fields, a single egret tries its wings.
Who would know my sailing on the misty Five Lakes for
      Fan Li?
He alone could forget the worldly scheme of things.

Su Wu's Temple

He knew, as the envoy of Han to the Mongols,
His life, the mission could cost.
Now before his old shrine and tall trees,
For words I feel lost.

Under the moon of the Tartar sky,
Over the clouds, wild geese could not pass.
He herded sheep at the border,
Amid mists and tall grass.

Before the Prime Curtain of the Royal Terrace,
Of recognition on return, he was bereft.
At the young age of twenty,
With the envoy's cap and sword, he lad left.

He was bestowed the seal of a Marquis,
A title that the spirit at Mouling could not see.
Facing fall waves, he wept in vain for his lost youth.
Like time, the stream cannot retract its journey.

Taking Leave of a Friend Going East

Yellow leaves are falling beyond the desolate frontiers,
But to leave the old country, you have made up your mind.
You will reach Ying Men Mountain by sunrise,
And in the high wind, leave the Han Yang Ferry behind.

In time, how many of us will still be here by the river?
From the horizon, your lone, returning sail will show.
When shall we meet again?
A cup of wine will soothe our parting woe.

Dreaming of the South Side of the River

After dressing, alone to the River Watching Tower go I.
By early morn, I lean to watch your homecoming ship.
A thousand boats have gone by.
You did not make this trip.
At sunset, quiet waters flow for many a mile,
Leaving me broken-hearted on White Duckweed Isle.

LI SHANGYIN (c813-858)

Ancient Zither

This ancient zither by chance has fifty strings,
Each to recall a blooming year's happenings.
At dawn, Chuangzi woke perplexed.
By his dream of the butterfly he was vexed.
At his death, King Wang's soul was reborn
Into a cuckoo, over faded springs, to weep and mourn.
Under the vast sea, with bright moonlight,
Pearls from teardrops could be in sight.
Under a warm sun, from every hill,
Many spots with mists, jade mines fill.
I can wait to recall what happens today.
Only by then my memory will be in disarray.

At Bei Jing Luo Monastery

The sun has gone down behind the western hills.
A lone monk in his thatched hut, I want to see.
Layers of cold clouds hide my path.
Amid falling leaves, where is he?

Alone at dusk, he strikes the musical stone.
Idly he leans on a single cane.
This world is just a speck of dust.
From love or hate, how can I not abstain?

At Choubi Post-House

Your dispatches on bamboo,
Birds and monkeys still solemnly regard.
Your palisades and borders,
Wind and cloud often guard.

The chief commander wrote an ingenious plan
In vain, for the kingdom they were to defend.
The king you served surrendered
And left on a courier cart in the end.

The talented statesmen, Guan Chong and Yue Yi,
Proved to be no disgrace compared with you.
Your brave generals, Guan Yu and Chang Fei,
Died in battle, but what could one do?

When I pass your shrine
Near Brocade City some year,
I shall chant your "Song of the Sacred Mountains",
Overcome by regret and despair.

Because...

More for the presence of a mica screen,
Her chamber shows infinite charm.
But in the capital, she dreads spring nights,
When it is just getting warm.

She has married a high official.
On the random choice of a mate, she bet.
Ungratefully, for the king's pre-dawn audiences,
He leaves her under the scented coverlet.

The Cicada

Your lofty nature makes it hard to fill your belly.
You voice your anguish with nothing to gain.
Then your few chirps taper off by the fifth watch,
On a green tree callous to your pain.

A petty officer like me drifts on water as a twig.
My fields at home are all weed-free.
You took the trouble to show your admonition.
My whole family will live by lofty standards though in
        poverty.

Climbing Loyu Plateau

Towards evening, feeling ill at ease,
On a carriage, I climb a plateau of the past.
The fine sunset can infinitely please,
But near dusk, it cannot last.

For the Official Ling Hu

Like the trees of Qin and the clouds of Song,
For long we are separated by where we stay,
Joined merely by the carps
That carry letters between us far away.

Do not ask about the guest
In Prince Liang's garden of the past.
I am like the ailing Xiangyu,
Amid Muling's rain and blast.

Jasper Pool

By Jasper Pool, Queen Mother opens her silk casement.
The sad song "Yellow Bamboos" gets the earth shaken.
His eight horses can cover thirty thousand miles a day.
A return trip why has King Mu not taken?

Moon Lady

Upon a mica screen, the candle casts a deep shadow.
The Milky Way slowly wanes, with dawn stars on the go.
Of her stolen elixir, the Moon Lady should repent,
Each night, over the green sea and blue sky, in woe.

To…

It is hard to meet each other,
Equally hard to part.
The east wind is waning.
A hundred flowers are falling apart.

The spring silkworm, until it dies,
Spins silk on and on.
The candle sheds its tears
Until all the wax is gone.

Looking into a mirror at dawn,
Over the changes of your cloud-like hair, you fret.
Chanting poetry by night,
The chill of moonlight I get.

My love, like a fairy at Penglai,
Stays not too far from me.
Blue Bird, please visit and get news from her.
My earnest messenger, you will be.

Spring Rain

In a white, lined robe, I lie ruefully in spring,
Reminded of my frustrations in Baimen in a string.
There, across the rain, your red pavilion is a chilly sight.
On my return alone, my beaded blind wavers with lamplight.

The long way home in spring should sadden me at sunset.
Before the night ends, a hazy dream of you I may still get.
Ear-rings and my letters to her, how do I send?
Through myriad miles of dense clouds, on a wild goose I
    depend.

A Sui Dynasty Palace

In the palace, who was there to heed the counsels?
The king toured the south for fun, with no security measure.
In the spring breeze, the whole country got busy weaving
    silk,
To make his saddle-flaps and sails, for show and pleasure.

Thoughts in the Cold

You left and a new flood levels with the sills.
Dews fill the branches and mute cicadas are seen.
I think of you in this season.
For a long while, on the railing I lean.

Spring is far away, so is the northern wain.
Your words from Nanling are slow reaching me.
I divine my fate in dreams, so distant from you.
I suspect you might have new company.

Untitled, no. 1

In the previous evening, there were stars.
A wind blew at night.
Between west of the painted pavilion
And east of the Cassia Hall, we did unite.

My body lacks the two wings
Of the colorful phoenix to fly to you.
But like the magic of a rhino's horn,
Our minds connect in one line through.

We sat and played the fishing game,
Sipping some warm spring wine.
Then in groups, we tried solving riddles
While brightly red candles did shine.

Alas! At the beat of the drum,
I was called for my court duties in town.
Hurriedly I rode to the Orchid Terrace,
Like a tumbleweed, uprooted and blown.

Untitled, no. 2

With the east wind comes a rain, fine and light.
Beyond the lotus pond, thunders sound faint and slight.
Into the censer, locked with a copper toad, incense is still fed.
Down the deep well with a jade tiger, pails by a rope can still
    be led.

At young Han Yuan, Jia's daughter peeped through her blind.
For the talented Prince of Wei, her pillow Lady Mi left
    behind.
From vying with spring blooms, let my amorous heart
    refrain.
For each inch of longings for you, just an inch of ash would
    remain.

Untitled, no. 3

You have left without a trace.
Empty is the promise you will appear.
On the tower falls slanting moonlight.
The fifth night-watch I hear.

I dreamed about your leaving on a long trip
Which my words and tears could not turn back.
Then, I write you a letter in haste
Before my ink gets thick and black.

On my emerald screen with gold inlays,
Dim candlelight is shed.
Through my bed-curtain with embroidered hibiscus,
The faint smell of musk is spread.

Master Liu met a fairy at the Immortals' mountain
And already lamented the long distance in his day.
Comparing myself with the fairy,
I am ten thousand times farther away.

Wind and Rain

I feel for myself, after reading the "Precious Sword" essay,
Being a drifter by the end of the year.
Yellow leaves still sway and swing in the wind and rain.
From rich houses, music from pipes and strings one can hear.

Class and caste cut me off from new friends.
For lack of luck, contacts with old friends I cannot remake.
The wine of Xinfeng is my heart's desire.
I shall rid my woe with it, whatever price it may take.

CHEN TAO (824-882)

Song of Long Si

To subdue the Huns, they swear to die.
Now beneath the foreign soil, five thousand men lie.
Each corpse by the Wuding River, what a pitiful sight,
In a chamber, is still her dream-lover at night.

WEI ZHUANG (836-910)

Despair
Tune: "Lotus Leaf Cup" (Ho Ye Bei)

Through the ages, she is a lady, pretty and rare,
An empire-wrecker, peerless and fair.
But dateless for a union, under flowers in despair,
With her sad brows like the far hills,
To further ponder over her woe, she cannot bear.

Behind a shut kingfisher screen with golden phoenixes, she
     is to spend
Idle time for dreams that wane and end.
From her empty, painted hall with silk drapes, it is hard to send
Her message across the blue, trackless sky.
To her doleful mind, in an old chamber, none can attend.

Impressions of Jinling

Amid an endless drizzle on the river with level sedges,
Birds vainly cry, but the dream-like Six Dynasties did not last.
By the palace walls, willows are the most callous.
Along the long dyke, veiled in mists, they thrive as in the past.

Lovesickness
Tune: "Sand of Silk-Washing Stream"
(Huan Chi Sha)

I wish to mount the swing, but my limbs are weak.
To get someone to push me, I am too meek.
Curtained within my painted hall from wind and moon, none
     I can seek.

I get most amorous - who would not tonight?
Over the wall, the snowy pear petals make a lovely sight.
My worn-out, pretty face keeps a blush ever so slight.

Night thoughts at Zhang Tai

Clear lute-notes of regret, lingering through the night,
Like a storm, sadly resound around the strings.
I hear the Chu horns alone under a lamp.
Behind Zhang Tai, the waning moon sinks.

Fragrant grasses have withered.
My old friend has not come.
My letters for my family do not get there.
Again, the autumn wild geese turn south for home.

Yearnings
Tune: "Sand of Silk-Washing Stream" (Huan Chi Sha)

I yearn for you by the water-clock through each night.
Heart-broken at the railing, I thought you might
Think of me in my old brocade quilt, under the bright moonlight.

Shut in my small, painted hall, deep like the sea.
When I think of you, I read your letters to me.
For us to enter Changan hand-in-hand, when will it be?

LI PIN (mid 9th century)

On Crossing the River Han

On the far side of the mountain, I received no words,
For one winter and then another spring.
Approaching home, I become quiet and more timid,
Over the kind of news the greeter may bring.

MA DAI (mid 9th century)

Autumn Hut by the River Ba

Wind and rain have stopped on the Ba Plain,
With busy lines of dusk wild-geese in flight.

Leaves fall from trees of a strange land.
Only a cold lamp is with me at night.

White dew drips in the empty garden.
The monk next door is socially detached and free.
For long I have lived in the outskirts.
To serve the country, which door will be open to me?

By the River Chu, Remembering the Past

While cold light and dew weave in the air,
The weak sun dropping behind the Chu hills is on the wane.
Monkeys screech in the trees by Dongting Lake.
In a magnolia boat, I remain.

A bright moon rises from the vast lake.
Wild torrents course down the dark mountain's height.
Unable to see the Spirit of the Clouds,
I grieve over autumn through the night.

CUI TU (late 9th century)

Reflections on New Year's Eve

On this distant Three Ba Road,
For myriad miles, I am tied to a perilous journey.
With flecks of snow on jagged hills at night,
In this strange land, I have none with me.

I get farther and farther away.
More intimate with servants, I gradually stay.
Besides, in my wandering and drifting life,
A new year will come the next day.

The Solitary Wild Goose

Lines of wild geese have vanished.
Where is this straggler heading, I wonder?
For your lost companions, you scream in the evening rain.
Whether to enter the cold pond alone, you ponder.

As you skim low in the dark, cloudy night,
Afar, the cold, frontier moon keeps you company.
You may not meet a fowler's arrow,
But on constant guard, the lone flier must be.

DU XINHE (late 9th century)

Grievance in the Spring Palace

Early I fell under the snare of feminine charm.
Now before the mirror, I loathe to do my face and hair.
My appearance delights the emperor no more.
How can I make myself look attractive and fair?

The high sun casts layers of shadows on flowers.
Birds are twittering in the warm, windy weather.
I think of my female companions by the Yue stream,
Year after year, plucking lotus flowers together.

HAN WU (late 9th century)

Already Cool

Beyond the green railing hangs the embroidered blind she
    displays.

Her scarlet screen is painted with floral sprays.
Her neat, brocade quilt is spread on a long, woven mat,
In this already cool weather before the really cold days.

QIN TAOYU (late 9th century)

The Poor Girl

I come from a humble home with a wicket gate.
To me, the good smell of silk and gauze is not yet known.
I plan to ask a good matchmaker to help me,
But feel more hurt by myself alone.

Who would appreciate my conduct of life?
In a high standard, this I maintain.
I feel for the hardship of making a living.
A habit of skimming on personal grooming I retain.

I dare boast my embroidery skills
From the ten deft fingers of mine.
I care not to compete with other girls,
On painted brows, in length and line.

I bitterly resent stitching gold threads for years on end.
Making wedding gowns for others, my back I bend.

ZHANG QIAO (late 9th century)

News from the Frontier

Bugle calls have stopped in autumn.
Against the Drum Tower, soldiers lean.

Spring winds pass over the green grave of Concubine Wang.
Having fallen in Liangzhou, the white sun cannot be seen.

War has ended beyond the frontier.
To the farthest borders, travelers can go.
I wish the Tibetans' allegiance is like this river,
Forever wishing to make its southward flow.

ZHANG BI (10th century)

For Someone

Back to your house, my dreams after leaving are sailing,
With its small corridor and zigzag railing.
The sentimental moon of my spring courtyard
Shines on the fallen petals, without failing.

LI YU (937-978)

Court Dancer

Already at a good height, the sun shines red.
Another bit of the beast-shaped incense to the copper censer
        is fed.
Wrinkles in the red brocade follow dance shoes that tread.

Her gold hairpin slips off in a dance display.
She sniffs the heart of a flower to drive her tipsiness away,
Hearing, from a distant palace, flutes and drums in play.

Lament
Tune: "Song of Ziye" (Zi Ye Ge)

Of woe and lament, how can one's life be free?
How limitless is the languor consuming just me?
In a dream, a trip to my old kingdom I make.
Tears fall down my cheek, when awake.
With whom did I climb the high tower together?
I long remember looking out with you in sunny, fall weather.
My past deeds have been in vain.
To a dream, they just pertain.

Longings
Tune: "Eternal Longing" (Chang Xiang Si)

Hills in one fold.
Hills in another fold.
Our longings stretch over far hills under a distant sky,
With mists over waters, and red maples in the cold.

Chrysanthemums open.
Chrysanthemums fade.
Wild geese fly high for home, but returning to me you deny.
Behind a screen under wind and moon, listless I am made.

Parting Grief
Tune: "Joy at Meeting" (Shuang Jian Huan)

I ascend the West Tower, mute and alone.
A sickle moon is shown.
A lone wutong tree stands there,
In the deep courtyard, locked in the cool autumn air.

My yearnings I cannot sever.
After sorting, they get more tangled ever.
Grief when we are apart
Leaves a special taste in my heart.

Regret
Tune: "Night Crow Calling" (Ye Ya Ti)

Vernal, red flowers of the woods do not last,
All too fast,
Vainly against the cold, dawn rain and evening blast.
By your tear-stained rouge, that day,
Drunk, I wanted to stay.
To repeat that, when shall we get?
Like the river always heading east, this is my life's lasting
regret.

Sorrow
Tune: "The Beautiful Lady Yu" (Yu Mei Ren)

Spring blooms and autumn moons - how long do they last?
How much has happened to me in the past?
On my small house, an east wind blew again last night.
I could not bear recalling my old kingdom in the bright
moonlight.
The carved railings and jade inlays should still be the
same,
Except the look of my favorite dame.
How much sorrow can you hold, may I know?
Mine is just like a river in spring in its eastward flow.

Woe
Tune: "Gathering the Mulberry" (Cai Sang Zi)

Red flowers perish when spring is driven away,
Lingering and dancing in the courtyard, here and there,
Amid a drizzle everywhere.
For now, I let my just loosened brows stay.

Floral fragrance ends at my green window, cold and still.
Into ashes, my incense slabs burn.
In a dream, my sad feelings return,
Entering my sleepy head against my will.

Yearnings
Tune: "Beautiful Lady Yu" (Yu Mei Ren)

Across the small, green courtyard, winds whirl and blow.
Throughout spring, new willow buds sprout and show.
I lean on the railing, alone and without a word.
Under the same old crescent moon, bamboo music I heard.
My cup of wine stands before me, with song and music
	around.
In the deep painted pavilion, with faint incense and a lit
	candle,
I find my temples full of snowflakes and yearnings hard to
	handle.

Upon Waking from a Dream

Beyond my screen, a drizzle does stay
On this late spring day.
Against the pre-dawn chill, my silken quilt cannot fight.
Of being a guest-prisoner, I dreamily lose sight,
Indulged in a fleeting moment of delight.

I shall not lean on a railing alone.
My old, boundless kingdom is gone.
Leaving it is easy;
Seeing it again is not meant to be.
Like fallen blooms, flown water and faded spring,
It belongs to Heaven, not an earthling.

LIU YONG (987-1053)

Longings
Tune: Feng Qi Wu

Inside a high tower, in the calm wind, I lean alone,
Sad over my lover having been gone.
I gaze at the edge of the gloomy sky
Where blurry grass and hill in the fading sun lie.
My feelings now at the railing are known by none.

On an uninhibited thought, I planned to drink hard,
Sing and for once get drunk off-guard.
But forced drinks give bad taste.
My belt is too loose for my thinning waist.
For her, I do not ever regret looking haggard.

Parting
Tune: Yu Lin Ling

Cicadas chirp, intense and sad, in the cold,
Before the tall pavilion at night,
Just after the halt of a sudden rain.
Outside the city, after some drinks we feel low.
In the parting place, we want to stay

But a waiting magnolia boat presses us to go.

There, our teary eyes meet as hands we hold
And words freeze.
To think - leaving am I,
Over a thousand miles of wave and mist,
Under low, dark clouds, for the broader, southern sky.
Over partings, since the old days, we are all in woe,
More unbearably on this cold and lonely fall day.

Sobering up today, I wonder where I exist -
At a river-bank where willows grow,
At night with a waning moon,
Or at dawn with a breeze.
I have left you for many a year,
Wasting all the good times and fine sceneries together.
Now if I could have a thousand tender thoughts to release,
With whom should I share?

OUYANG XIU (1007-1072)

Memory
Tune: "Gazing at the South" (Wang Jiang Nan)

South of the river stands a willow,
With no shade from its small leaves to show.
Who bears to break its light, silky twigs?
Too tender now to support a singing oriole,
Deeper into springtime, stronger it will grow.

A fourteen- or fifteen-year-old looked high and low.
With a pipa, she passed below.
On the steps, we gambled.
I already left my heart in her that long ago.
Right now, how can it not be so?

Regret
Tune: "Ripples Sifting Sand" (Lang Tao Sha)

To East Wind, a toast for you from me.
I plead for your presence, unhurried and free.
Visiting the purple banks under a drooping willow tree,
East of Luoyang, hand-in-hand,
We toured all the scented woods completely.

We met and quickly you left me.
An endless regret, it will be.
This year's flowers are redder than last, we agree.
But next year's flowers will do better still.
Who will be my partner then? What a pity!

West Lake
Tune: "Picking the Mulberry" (Cai Sang Zi)

I cruise with wine on a pleasure boat,
On West Lake for a fine float,
With fast music from pipes and strings
And quick passing of wine cups and things,
On the calm waves and let go for a drunken sleep.

Yet trailing under our moving boat, the clouds keep.
The whole atmosphere
Looks fresh and clear.
High and low, I linger to explore
And fancy another world at its core.

The Thrush

With many a chirp and trill,
The thrush moves at will

Among purple and red flowers that show
From branches high and low.
Until now I begin to see,
Only on woodlands free,
Not a cage, would a bird
Make better songs to be heard.

SU SHI (1037-1101)

Drunk again after Sobering up, by the East Slope
Tune: "Immortals by the River" (Lin Jiang Xian)

Around the third watch, my way home I found.
My snoring houseboy was making a thunderous sound,
And deaf to the door on which I did pound.

I long regret my living body without a free will is in a bind.
With whom can I blot this busy life off my mind?
Into the night, ripples look smooth in the calm wind.

From here, on a small boat, I shall be on my way,
To rest my mind on river and sea, each remaining day.

During the Mid-Autumn Festival
Tune: "Prelude to Water Music"
(Shui Diao Guo Tiao)

When is the moon fully bright?
I ask of the blue sky, wine in hand.
In the palaces of Heaven, I do not know
What season of the year it is tonight.
Riding the wind, I wish I could get there,

But in the jade mansions at a great height,
The cold, I fear I cannot stand.
In the light, I rise to dance and play with my lone shadow.
How unlike being on mortals' land!

Sailing around your red pavilion, the moonlight
Shines low through your draped window,
Keeping you awake.
No grudge you should show.
Only with us apart, why is there always a full moon in sight?
The moon may wax, wane, dim or glow.
Humans may grieve, gladden, part or unite.
About life's imperfections through the ages we know.
May we all live for many a year.
Over myriad miles, the same moon together we share.

Memories of the Past at the Red Cliff
Tune: "The Charm of Niannu" (Nian Nu Jiao)

For myriad years, the big river's eastward flow,
On its waves, has scoured all the way
The gallant people of their day.
Near the old ramparts, on the west side,
People say,
Stands the Red Cliff of Zhou Yu of the Three Kingdoms
        still.
Clouds get cracked up by jumbled rocks.
Waves pound the shores with fearful shocks,
Rolling up like a thousand drifts of snow.
The picturesque river and hill
Once set the stage for many a hero.

I recall, years ago,
Younger Miss Qiao just married Zhou Yu,
In style and action, a hero.
With a feathered fan and a silk headdress,

Laughing as he spoke,
He burned his rival's mast and oar up into flying ash and
      smoke.
My mind tours the old kingdoms inside.
My sentimentality you should deride
And my young hair graying so.
The human world is like a dream.
Let me make a libation to the moon in-stream.

Caught in the Rain
Tune: Ding Feng Bo

Do not hear the sound on forest leaves from each spatter and
      blow.
Why not chant and leisurely go?
Compared with a horse, light are my straw sandals and a
      bamboo cane.
Who is afraid?
A straw rain-cloak against a life of mist and rain.

From a stupor, the cold spring wind wakes me.
Somewhat chilly.
But from the hills, greeting me are slanting sunbeams.
I turn my head towards the bleak terrain.
Head back again.
On me, no effects can wind, rain or sunshine show.

Secret Love
Tune: "Butterflies Lingering over Flowers"
(Die Lian Hua)

The red hue of wilting flowers does not last.
Green apricots are small.
When swallows fly,

Near homes, green waters wind their ways around.
Fewer catkins stay on willow branches after another blast.
Everywhere on this land, scented grasses can still be found.

I am the passer-by.
A fair lady laughs inside.
Then her peals of laughter go mute as the noises slowly
      subside.
I am vexed that the amorous feelings I want to confide
Is met by her callousness, as if to brush me aside.

Spring Night

Each moment of a spring night is priceless.
From the terrace, the pitch of songs and pipes go light,
With a soothing aroma from flowers, a misty moon
And her swing in the courtyard, deep into the night.

To my Dead Wife
Tune: Jiang Cheng Zi

Ten years have long passed between the living and the dead,
A thought not dwelled on in my head,
But a natural memory hard to shed.
In a lonely grave, a thousand miles away,
You are not here to share my woe.
Even if we met today,
My dusty face you should not know,
With temple hair like snow.

In a dream of home-coming last night,
In your small room, through a window,
Of you on your toilet, I caught sight.
After a mutual gaze, we had no speech or sound,

But a thousand lines of tears rolling down.
Each year, I expect a gut-wrenching round,
Visiting you under bright moonlight,
At the dwarf pine-clad mound.

The West Lake when Rain is Falling

In the sun, lake waters gleam with a sheen.
In the rain, the hills look misty and rare.
Heavily adorned or not, it looks just right,
Like the famed beauty, Si Shi, if we want to compare.

Written on the Wall of Xilin Monastery

A ridge across to my eyes, but a peak in side-view,
From each distance or angle, the scene is new.
Just because I am within the mountain range,
I do not know the real face of Mount Lu.

QIN GUAN (1049-1110)

The Cowherd Star and the Weaver Maid
Tune: "Immortals at the Magpie Bridge"
(Que Aiao Xian)

Through thin clouds, in a pretty array,
Messages of regrets shooting stars convey.
The Cowherd Star and the Weaver Maid
Secretly cross the long Milky Way.
The lovers' meeting in the sky only once a year
Means more than our many unions down here.

Their love and tenderness like water seem;
Their splendid union, a dream.
Unbearable it is to watch and learn
On the Magpie Bridge they must return.
But if their mutual love is enduring and right,
What matters if they do not meet each day and night?

A Long, Cold Night
Tune: "As in a Dream" (Ru Meng Ling)

Like water, the long night stands still.
A strong wind shuts the post-station tight.
I have a broken dream tonight.
A mouse peeps at my light.
My padded quilt fails to fight
The frost that sends the morning chill.
Sleepless I stay.
Sleepless I stay.
People rise and outside horses neigh.

LI QINGZHAO (1081-1143)

Lady on a Swing
Tune: "Painting Crimson Lips" (Dian Jiang Qun)

After playing on a swing, she stands
And flexes her delicate hands.
Flowers shrivel in the dense dew.
With a thin sweat, her light dress is soaked through.

She sees someone coming around.
Her gold hairpin slips off and stockings fall down.

Abashed, she runs but leans at the door to look back,
Sniffing green plums for the scent they lack.

Autumn Festival
Tune: "Tipsy under Flowers" (Zui Hua Yin)

I spend a misty and cloudy day with lasting woe.
In my beast-shaped, copper censer, the incense burns low.
A fine Autumn Festival falls on this day.
I rest on a jade pillow, inside my gauze net.
All over me, the first midnight chill I get.

Wine in hand, by the east fence, at night,
I can smell, through my sleeves, a sweet scent ever so light.
Who can deny this soul-thrilling power?
With my blinds rolled up, in the west wind I stay,
Looking weaker than a yellow flower.

Flowers from a Peddler
Tune: "Magnolia Blooms, Short Form"
(Jian Ze Mu Lan Hua)

From the flowers that the peddlers bring,
I bought a spray about to bloom in spring.
Spread light and even, the tear drops of morning dew
Still make marks on the petals with a crimson hue.

He may guess and say, I am afraid,
When a contest is made,
My face against a flower is less fair.
With a hairpin aslant on my cloud-like hair,
Against all odds, I would still ask him to compare.

Grief

For you I look and look,
Alone and chilled,
My heart sinking with sorrow filled.

The fair weather was a tease.
Now I rest not in peace.
Sips of wine at night
Quell not the blast and its might.

A wild goose has flown,
The same bird from the old days that I have known.
On the ground, yellow flowers heap,
Weak and weary.
Who will pick them up to keep?

I wait alone by day at the window.
To pass into night, time seems slow.
Towards dusk starts a light rain,
On my tree, dripping now and again.

These sights and sounds, one by one -
How heart-breaking they are, to my belief,
And how inept is just the word "grief"!

Fisherman's Pride

In the sky, a dawn fog and billowy clouds unite.
On the River of Stars, about to churn,
A thousand sails are set to dance and turn.
To God's place, in a dream, my soul seems to return.
From Heaven, I hear an earnest query
About my route and destiny.
I say, "On life's long road, short is my time.
As a student of poetry, I lack lines astounding and prime."

The roc, with its wings just raised,
For myriad miles, takes a windy flight.
Wind, do not stop.
Blow my humble boat to the Three Hills' height.

By the Brook
Tune: "As in a Dream" (Ru Meng Ling)

I keenly remember by the brook at the end of the day.
Drunk by the arbor, we lost our way.
Late but all cheered, for the boat we did make
And sail into the deep of lotus blooms by mistake.
To get across, we fought.
To get across, we fought.
The havoc of rising, startled herons we brought.

The Rain Last Night
Tune: "As in a Dream" (Ru Meng Ling)

In the scattered rain last night,
I slept sound and tight,
As the wind suddenly blew.
Now my morning hangover is not through.

The shade someone does fold
And reply, "Your cherry-apple tree is the same as old."
I say, "Don't you know?
Don't you know?
Red petals should thin out and green, fat leaves grow."

Alone
Tune: "As in a Dream" (Ru Meng Ling)

Who is my partner when sitting alone by a bright window?

Two people, summing me and my shadow.
Under a burnt lamp, when I am sleepy,
My shadow will also be on the go.
Help me.
Help me.
A poignant picture of me in woe.

Lantern Festival
Tune: "Joy of Eternal Union" (Yong You Luo)

Like molten gold, sets the sun.
Like pieces of jade, dusk clouds join into one.
But where is he?
A dense fog soaks up the willow.
Flute music to "Falling Plum Petals" brings woe.
What signs of spring are known to me?
The Lantern Festival is here,
With warm and agreeable weather.
But of wind and rain, is it already clear?
For a get-together,
I thank them for a horse-drawn carriage, scented and fine,
To attend their wine-and-poetry party, which I decline.

The capital saw days of prosperity and pleasure.
As a girl, I had much leisure.
The Lantern Festival was my favorite, I recall.
With a kingfisher cap on my head,
And a "snow-willows" ornament in golden thread,
I fought to look the best of all.
Now looking haggard,
With frosted and wind-blown hair,
I fear my having a night out would be a social hazard.
I would rather face the bottom of my blind, for that matter,
And hear the festival-goers' laughs and chatter.

Lament at Night
Tune: "Butterflies Lingering over Flowers"
(Die Lian Hua)

All through this boring night with little delight,
I dream of Changan in vain.
On the road to Changan, I should think,
Partaking in this year's fine spring scene,
The flowers and the moon should well emit a sheen

Off something casual, I dine,
With sour plums and good wine,
Just suiting me fine.
Flower, jeer not at my putting a bloom in my hair while tipsy.
Just pity spring will age like me.

Longing for My Lover
Tune: Yi Chien Mei

The red, scented blooms of lotus fade,
In autumn on a mat of jade.
With my gauze dress lightly set free,
I board a boat alone.
From the clouds, who sent a letter to me?
When wild geese return,
The West Chamber will be under full moonlight.

Fallen petals drift with the water in its flow.
The same longings between you and me
Become sadness in two places, left idle and free.
I have no clues to rid this woe.
From my brows, it is to depart,
Yet creeping up to my heart.

Sorrow
Tune: "Happy Events Approaching" (Hao Shi Jin)

Under a still wind, fallen blooms pile deep.
Beyond my blind, red petals and white snow heap.
I long remember the scene after crabapples blossoming at
    their prime.
Seeing spring on its wane gives me a pitiful time.

After all the drinking and singing are done,
My jade goblet is an empty one,
And my flickering lamp will be gone.
In a dream or awake, already I cannot bear sheltered sorrow,
And a call of the cuckoo makes it more unbearably so.

ZHAO JI (r 1101-1125)

To Apricot Blossoms

Like tailored silk, the petals are molded,
Clear and icy thin,
In layers lightly folded,
Casually and evenly rouged in.
With pretty make-up in new style glowing,
And fragrance melted in beauty overflowing,
Your presence makes palace ladies die in shame.

Easily the petals are on the wane.
After how many heartless pelts of wind and rain,
With how much sorrow and pain,
In the courtyard bleak and cold,
For how many late, spring days can you sustain?

To Swallows

For leaving my old kingdom, after I depart,
My regrets with two swallows I share.
But the deep feelings from my heart,
In human tongue, they cannot know or care.

In a faraway land, under a distant sky,
Over many a river or hill,
Where does the old palace lie?
Where is it still?

The past, can one not recall?
At times, my dreams of the palace old
Leave no memories at all.
In dreams of late, the past is on hold.

YUE FEI (1103-1142)

The River Runs Red

Anger makes me bristle
And my hat rise.
Leaning on the railing,
In a halt of the rushing rain,
I look up
And howl for long at the sky,
Greatly agitated by my strong emotions inside.
After age thirty came my fame, like dust and soil,
Under cloud and moon, through eight thousand miles of toil.
Do not tarry.
When my young hair turns gray,
I shall grieve in vain.

In Jingkang's reign, the shame over our military failing

Has to be avenged yet.
As a general, when can this regret
Be wiped off and cast aside?
On a long chariot, I will harass,
Stamp and break the enemy at the Mount Helan Pass.
In high spirits, the barbarian flesh we will hungrily eat,
Amid laughs and chatter, with Tartar blood for a thirst-
        quenching treat.
Let me start over to recapture the lost territory
For our majesty.

LU YOU (1125-1210)

Ambition
Tune: Ye You Gong

Dawn breaks in the snow,
With the shrill and chaotic sound of the Tartar pipe.
In my dream, on a trek unknown,
Mute like water, my armed cavalry was on the go,
Past a frontier river,
West of the Yen Mountain,
By Qinghai.

In my bed, as the cold lamp is spent
And the water-clock becomes silent,
With moonlight aslant through my paper window,
I recall my ambition to make a name,
Through victories myriad miles away.
Who would know,
Though my temple hair has turned gray,
My heart is still after fame.

Awakening
Tune: "Spring in Han Palace" (Han Gong Chun)

With feathered arrows and a carved bow,
Atop the ancient rampart, I remember,
Calling my falcon and confronting a tiger,
On the vast, level plain.
I returned to my tent at twilight,
At the blare of the Tartar pipe,
With my green blanket under the weight of snow.

Then I freely wrote in drunken delight,
With lines like dragons and snakes in flight,
Landing on Tartar paper rolls.
They over-praised me
For my military strategy and heartfelt poetry,
Besides excellent prowess and energy.

Now on some matter, to the south I go.
Of the Double Ninth Herb Market, I take in the sight.
Like hills, the high lanterns glow,
In this festival of the first full moonlight.
At the fireworks, the huge crowd cheers with glee.
I let my whip hang, my cap askew.
The singing reminds me of the days gone by.
Before the wine cup, I cry.

Take this to heart:
Rank and status depend on how you achieve.
Merit and fame come not from Heaven, to my belief.

Complaint
Tune: Shuang Tou Lian

Like stars, my temple hair turns white.
To nil, I fear my grand ambitions have gone.

I just exist and hang on,
Like a sick horse, desolate and alone.
In the dark, on my own,
All dissipated is my former, undaunted spirit of a hero.

My hometown, with many a hill and stream,
Over layers of mists and water,
Gets lost in my broken dream.
I am ten thousand miles away.
My old friends vanish.
Who remembers the visits to the Green Gate?

Chengdu prospers, they all say.
I sigh at being idle during work hours that go slow.
Into sleeping more at home, I am sunk.
To cleanse my woe, by myself I get drunk.

Right now, I reckon
For unloading my concerns, to whom can I go?
Even if a rudder from Chu and a mast from Wu were mine,
The time I could sail east, who would know?
In vain, I pine
For good fish and fragrant mushrooms.
When again will rise the winds of fall?

Fisherman's Delight
Tune: "Immortals at the Magpipe Bridge"
(Que Qiao Xian)

I indulged in gambling under a splendid lamp's glow.
On an engraved saddle, I shot and rode in speed.
Who remembers the past and each grandiose deed?
To seek office, one by one, all drinkers go,
Except me.
By the river, I would rather a fisherman be.

In an eight-foot boat, long and light,
With lowered awnings in three,
I take over and enjoy the whole sight.
For people of leisure, Mirror Lake was set up and deemed
        right,
Without the need of any favor the court may bestow.

Hearing the Cuckoo at Night
Tune: "Immortals at the Magpie Bridge"
(Que Qiao Xian)

Under my thatched roof, none makes a sound.
Near the window, the lantern hardly emits a glow.
Wind and rain come over the river in this spring night.
Mute is every forest oriole or nesting swallow,
Except that under the moonlit sky,
Frequently goes a cuckoo's cry.

My tears of solitude hasten to flow.
I wake from a lonely dream with fright.
Deep into the woods, the cuckoo flies away.
Already in the hills of my hometown,
I could not bear to hear the call,
Especially now,
After drifting half my life.

Instruction to My Son

After death, to nothing all will go.
My divided country is my only woe.
When we have won over the northern rebels,
At my memorial, do not forget to let your father know.

My Faraway Hometown
Tune: You Jia Ao

Looking east, where is my hometown,
Thirteen thousand miles away, to and fro?
In full pages, I write home in vain.
My tears flow,
With no reply until a new year comes around.

The water under the Red Bridge please relay
My wish to seek my brothers, on a flat boat.
When is the day?
Sailing to the sky's edge, I have really aged so.
Sleepless, in woe.
Amid tea mists are the few threads of temple hair that
        remain.

My Philosophy of Life
Tune: "Partridge Sky" (Che Gu Tian)

Home is where green mists and sunsets are found.
To care about worldly affairs, I am no longer bound.
Emptying wine, I walk through the bamboo grove.
After reading "Huang Ting", I look at the hills while lying
        down.

I whistle with my head held high.
Worn and weak, I let my body grow.
I smile, why not, wherever I go.
The Creator makes his own plans, for long I know.
My old mind pays no heed to a hero.

To Plum Blossoms
Tune: "Song of Divination" (Bu Suan Zi)

By a broken bridge, outside a courier post,
It blossoms aimlessly alone,
Well into the evening, in sad solitude,
Being rain-soaked and wind-blown.

For the bitter battle of spring, it makes no wish,
Nor will the jealousy of other flowers rest on its mind.
Though ground into mud and dust,
Unchanged is its fragrance lingering behind.

Traveling by Boat along the Fan River

Why not take fine ferns and herbs as a traveler's fare?
I rap at a farmhouse door at sundown.
In the first autumn cold, short is my hair.
Bleak are the empty valleys around.

Famine occurs again this year.
Through the smartweed banks, my boat does tear,
Startling wild geese that rise to flee.
Calling cows home, by misty ponds, pipes blare.

Feelings expressed in poetry come only through poverty.
Even with setbacks and stumbles in life, it is not bad to be.

Unfulfilled Ambitions
Tune: "Telling of Innermost Feelings"
(Su Zhong Qing)

That year, on horseback I came
To the Liangzhou border, myriad miles away,
For fortune and fame.

After battles at passes and rivers unknown,
A broken dream is all I own.
Dusty and dark, my old sable coat has grown.

To wipe out the Tartars, I did fail.
Already my temple hair has turned gray,
And my shed tears are to no avail.

The future course of my life, who can decide?
To the Tian Shan frontier, my heart is tied,
But by the sylvan waterside, my body will age and reside.

XIN QIJI (1140-1207)

Looking for Her in the Lantern Festival
Tune: "Jade Green Cup" (Qing Yu An)

At night, a thousand lanterns hang from trees like flowers.
Then the east wind makes the sparks drop,
Like stars raining in a sheet.
Rare horses pull carved carriages on a fully scented street.
Flutes sound in full play.
Shadows move in the moon's pathway,
In a night of the Fish-Dragon Dance display.

Talking and laughing, with a wisp of perfume, dressed in
    gold,
Passing ladies don ornaments for all to behold,
Shaped in a moth or a snowy willow, on their hair.
I look for her many times and most everywhere,
Until my head takes a sudden turn,
To see her stop,
Where some lanterns at a railing still burn.

Written on the Wall in the Boshan Temple
Tune: "Ugly Servant" (Chou Nu Er)

Grief in my youth was not known.
I loved to climb on high,
I loved to climb on high,
Forced grief on my new verses to convey.

Grief to me now is well known.
My urge to talk, I deny,
My urge to talk, I deny,
But remark on a fine, cool autumn day.

JIANG JIE (1245-1310)

Listening to the Rain
Tune: "Beautiful Lady Yu" (You Mei Ren)

I listened to the rain in my younger days,
In a hall with a songstress for my delight.
Red candles cast their rays
On my silk bed-curtain at night.

I listened to the rain as a grown man in my prime,
A traveler on a boat-ride.
Above the wide river, clouds hung low at that time.
In the west wind, a stray wild goose cried.

Now I am listening to the rain in a monk's hut.
Like stars, specks of my white temple hair already show.
To the woe of partings and joy of meetings, my feelings are
     shut.
I just let the rain drip before my steps till the morrow.

MA JIYUAN (c1260-c1324)

Autumn Thoughts
Tune: "Sky Clear Sand" (Tian Jing Sha)

At dusk, on a dead vine of an old tree is a crow.
Families live near a small bridge and water in its flow.
A lean horse on an ancient road takes the west wind's blow.
Far on the horizon, the sun sinks low,
With a broken-hearted man in woe.

GUAN DAOSHENG (1262-1319)

To My Husband

Our mutual words and deeds of tenderness,
Our sentiments in excess,
And our abundance in love and desire,
Feel like a hot fire.

A lump of clay I hold.
A figurine of you I mold.
A likeness of me I also make.
Then together both objects I break.

I knead a new figurine of you, from the broken clay
And sculpt another of me, in the same way.
I shall then have my clay in you
And yours in mine too.

In life, we shall be under one coverlet;
In death, in the same casket.

LIU XIAOZU (fl. 1550)

To My Lover
Tune: Chao Tian Zi

Cherish a flower like me.
Love a flower like me.
A blink of the eye and spring may flee.
Suddenly I think of my cute enemy.
From him, not for a moment, can I be free.

Under the moon, we casually flirt and woo.
By the pillow, secret talks we do.
How come you treat them all like jokes between us two?
Do not show off my love for you.
A slick lover is my label for you.
Till death, I am not willing to be through.

XUE LUNDAO (fl. 1580)

Angry at the World
Tune: "Song of Water Nymph" (Sui Xian Zi)

On too torrid and frigid days,
Under churning clouds and pelting rain,
Dirty and hard, they make ways
In the battlefields, for fame and gain.

By the contentious seashore,
Where giant waves pile high,
Under smiles, they hide in store,
Swords and spears that lie.

Faking kindness,
They gossip at your back.
Everyone is a prey in the race,
Like the elephant swallowed by the snake,
The roebuck chased away by the hare
And dog-meat, instead of mutton, hung at the rack.

Mr. Goody-Goody

I

The long and short of others rest not on me.
Let their rights and wrongs be.
My three-inch tongue is clamped tight
To avoid a big calamity.
Why would I jabber outright?
I bow and say "yes" yielding to most I see,
For joining the in-crowd of society.

II

Do not say who is short and who is long.
Do not say who is right and who is wrong.
Nodding to agree in idle talks, be ready.
In contentions, pretend the wine you took is heady.
Lower your brows and shut your eyes, for another way.
Just with whomever, go along.
Stop grinding your teeth and wasting your words, right away.

NALAN XINDE (1655-1685)

Confession
Tune: "Picking the Mulberry" (Cai Sang Zi)

I made a mistake and now I say.
My sad thoughts run astray.
Secretly, my blood and tears fall.
Everything is amiss on this breezy, spring day.

I lack the means to return and surely I know.
I just promised a happy reunion for show.
Now we are so stuck being apart.
Pear flowers have all fallen and westwards the moon will go.

Lament
Tune: "Sand of Silk-Washing Stream" (Huan Xi Sha)

Wandering is pitiful, who can deny?
The same, old season of fair flowers comes by,
A year since broken-hearted you die.

As if rained on, in a patch of hazy red, flowers are found.
With mists, a few soft willow twigs just get bound.
Your beautiful soul ended before sundown.

Homesickness
Tune: "Eternal Longing" (Chang Xiang Ci)

Each hilly trip.
Each way by ship.

Towards Elm Pass we go.
Deep into the night,
A thousand tent-lights glow.

Each night-watch round.
Each snowy blast can hound
And wreck my dream of home at night.
Such ear-splitting sound
Never in my hometown is found.

A Listless Life
Tune: "Picking the Mulberry" (Cai Sang Zi)

Who is playing a sad song?
The wind is whistling.
The rain is whistling.
Again I watch my lamp go out, all night long.

What is tying my mind down?
Awake, I am listless.
Drunk, I am listless.
Again I dream without reaching my lover's town.

Loneliness
Tune: "Picking the Mulberry" (Cai Sang Zi)

The bright moon should laugh at my sentimentality
For being lonely and idle today,
And after amorous hearts I betray,
Chanting and walking on my way.

Of late, I fear talking about the past.
With casual friends I team.
As my candle burns low under pale moonbeams,
Where do I find my lover and haven in my dreams?

Sorrow
Tune: Tai Chang Yin

On flowers like bells, a night wind does pound.
In the Blue Hills Tower, I stick around,
Too sad to stand the sound.
Unbearable is the added din of springs and rain coming
    down.

Trackless and clueless, idle thoughts I address.
To whom should I convey my emotion in excess?
Even my dreams are in a mess.
Why wake me up from a dream in progress?

Wanderer's Woe
Tune: "Deva-like Barbarian" (Pu Sha Man)

Near mid-winter, a startling gale sweeps the ground.
My saddle gets unbridled, as twilight ravens move around.
Into one joined block, the ice turns the big river-flow,
And forms a vast expanse of sorrow.

At the edge of the scarred, scorched earth, I vainly stare.
Upon a high wall, drums resound and horns blare.
I shall be near Changan the next day.
The grief of a wanderer's heart has not gone away.

Index of Authors

Anonymous
    Ballad of Mulan   11
    Book of Songs   2
    Nineteen Ancient Poems   4
Bai Juyi   55
Bao Zhao   10
Cen Zhen   42
Chen Tao   79
Chen Ziang   15
Cui Hao   53
Cui Hu   63
Cui Shu   52
Cui Tu   82
Dai Shulun   49
Du Fu   36
Du Mu   67
Du Qiuniang   67
Du Xinhe   83
Gao Shi   43
Guan Daosheng   113
Han Hong   45
Han Wu   83
He Zhizhang   14
Ji Wuqian   46
Jia Dao   62
Jiang Jie   112
Li Bai   28
Li Pin   81
Li Qi   44
Li Qingzhao   97
Li Shangyin   72
Li She   63
Li Shen   63
Li Yi   65
Li Yu   85
Liu Fangping   65
Liu Shenxu   52

Liu Xiaozu   114
Liu Yong   89
Liu Yuxi   54
Liu Zhangqing   46
Liu Zhongyong   66
Liu Zongyuan   60
Lu Lun   45
Lu You   105
Ma Dai   81
Ma Jiyuan   113
Nalan Xinde   116
Ouyang Xiu   90
Qin Guan   96
Qin Taoyu   84
Shen Chuanqi   14
Su Shi   92
Tao Qian   6
Wang Changling   22
Wang Han   41
Wang Wei   23
Wang Xizhi   6
Wang Zhihuan   16
Wei Yingwu   50
Wei Zhuang   79
Wen Tingyun   70
Xie Lingyun   8
Xin Qiji   111
Xue Lundao   114
Yuan Jie   48
Yuan Zhen   61
Yue Fei   104
Zhang Bi   85
Zhan Fangsheng   9
Zhang Ji   54
Zhang Jiuling   15
Zhang Qiao   84
Zhao Ji   103
Zhu Qingyu   64
Zu Yong   43

Appendix: Chinese Texts

詩經 (Book of Songs)
關雎　p.2
關關雎鳩，在河之州。窈窕淑女，君子好逑。
參差荇菜，左右流之。窈窕淑女，寤寐求之。
求之不得，寤寐思服。悠哉悠哉，輾轉反側。
參差荇菜，左右采之。窈窕淑女，琴瑟友之。
參差荇菜，左右芼之。窈窕淑女，鐘鼓樂之。

靜女　p.2
靜女其姝，俟我于城隅。愛而不見，搔首踟躕。靜女其
孌，貽我彤管。彤管有煒，說懌女美。自牧歸荑，洵美
且異。匪女之為美，美人之貽。

桃夭　p.3
桃之夭夭，灼灼其華。之子于歸，宜其室家。
桃之夭夭，有蕡其實。之子于歸，宜其家室。
桃之夭夭，其葉蓁蓁。之子于歸，宜其家人。

草蟲　p.3
喓喓草蟲，趯趯阜蟲。未見君子，憂心忡忡。未即見止
，亦即覯止，我心則降。陟彼南山，言採其蕨。未見君
子，憂心惙惙。亦即覯止，我心則說。陟彼南山，言採
其薇。未見君子，我心傷悲。亦即見止，亦即覯止，我
心則夷。

古詩十九首 (Nineteen Ancient Poems)
迢迢牽牛星　p.4
迢迢牽牛星，皎皎河漢女。纖纖擢素手，札札弄機杼
。終日不成章，泣涕零如雨。河漢清且淺，相去復幾許
。盈盈一水間，脈脈不得語。

青青河畔草　　p.5
青青河畔草，鬱鬱園中柳。盈盈樓上女，皎皎當窗牖。
娥娥紅粉妝，纖纖出素手。昔為倡家女，今為蕩子婦。
蕩子行不歸，空床難獨守。

行行重行行　　p.5
行行重行行。與君生別離。相去萬餘里，各在天一涯。
道路阻且長，會面安可知。胡馬依北風，越鳥巢南枝。
相處日已遠，衣帶日已緩。浮雲蔽白日，遊子不顧返。
思君令人老，歲月忽已晚。棄捐勿復道，努力加餐飯。

王羲之 Wang Xizhi
蘭亭　　p.6
仰視碧天際，俯瞰淥水濱。寥闃無涯觀，寓目理自陳。
大矣造化工，萬殊莫不均。群籟雖參差，適我無非新。

陶潛 Tao Qian
飲酒　　p.6
結廬在人境，而無車馬喧。問君何能爾，心遠地能偏。
採菊東籬下，悠然見南山。山氣日夕佳，飛鳥相與還。
此中有真意，欲辨已忘言。

歸田園居，其一　　p.7
少無適俗韻，性本愛丘山。誤落塵網中，一去三十年。
羈鳥戀舊林，池魚思故淵。開荒南野際，守拙歸田園。
方宅十餘畝，草屋八九間。榆柳陰後簷，桃李羅堂前。
曖曖遠人村，依依圩里煙。狗吠深巷中，雞鳴桑樹顛。
戶庭無塵雜，虛室有餘閑。久在樊籠裏，復得返自然。

歸田園居，其五　　p.7
悵恨獨策還，崎嶇歷榛曲。山澗清且淺，可以濯吾足。
濾我新熟酒，隻雞招近局。日入室中闇，荊薪代明燭。
歡來苦夕短，已復至天旭。

謝靈運 Xie Lingyun
夜發石關亭　　p.8
隨山踰千里，浮溪將十夕。鳥歸息舟楫，星闌命行役。
亭亭曉月暎，泠泠朝露滴。

於南山往北山經湖中瞻眺　　p.8
朝旦發陽崖，景落憩陰峰。捨舟眺迴渚，停策依茂松。
側逕既窈窕，環洲亦玲瓏。俛視喬木杪，仰聆大壑灇。
石橫水分流，林密蹊絕蹤。解作竟何感，升長皆豐容。
初篁苞綠籜，新蒲含紫茸。海鷗戲春岸，天雞弄和風。
撫化心無厭，覽物眷彌重。不惜去人遠，但恨莫與同。
孤遊非情歎，賞廢理誰通。

湛方生 Zhan Fangsheng
還都帆　　p.9
高岳萬丈峻，長湖千里清。白沙窮年潔，林松冬夏青。
水無暫停流，木有千載貞。寤言賦新詩，忽忘羈客情。

帆入南湖　　p.10
彭蠡紀三江，廬岳主眾阜，白沙淨川路，青松蔚巖首。
此水何時流，此山何時有，人運互推遷，茲器獨長久。
悠悠宇宙中，古今迭先後。

鮑照 Bao Zhao
登廬山　　p.10
懸裝亂水區，薄旅次山楹。千巖盛阻積，萬壑勢迴縈。
龍崇高昔貌，紛亂襲前名。洞澗窺地脈，聳樹隱天經。
松磴上迷密，雲竇下縱橫。陰冰實夏結，焱樹信冬榮。
嘈囋晨鵾思，叫嘯夜猿清。深崖伏化蹟，穹岫閟長靈。
乘此樂山性，重以遠遊情。方躋羽人途，永與煙霧并。

無名氏 Anonymous
木蘭詞　　p.11

唧唧復唧唧，木蘭當戶織。不聞機杼聲，唯聞女嘆息。
問女何所思，問女何所憶。女亦無所思，女亦無所憶。
昨夜見軍帖，可汗大點兵，軍書十二卷，卷卷有爺名。
阿爺無大兒，木蘭無長兄，願為市鞍馬，從此替爺征。
東市買駿馬，西市買鞍韉，南市買轡頭，北市買長鞭。
旦辭爺娘去，暮宿黃河邊。不聞爺娘喚女聲，但聞黃河
流水鳴濺濺。旦辭黃河去，暮至黑山頭。不聞爺娘喚女
聲，但聞燕山胡騎鳴。萬里赴戎機，關山度若飛。朔氣
傳金柝，寒光照鐵衣。將軍百戰死，壯士十年歸。歸來
見天子，天子坐明堂。策勳十二轉，賞賜百千疆。可汗
問所欲，木蘭不用尚書郎，願馳千里足，送兒還故鄉。
爺娘聞女來，出郭相扶將。阿姊聞妹來，當戶理紅妝。
小弟聞姊來，磨刀霍霍向豬羊。開我東閣門，坐我西間
床。脫我戰時袍，著我舊時裳。當窗理雲鬢，對鏡貼花
黃。出門看伙伴，伙伴皆驚惶。同行十二年，不知木蘭
是女郎。雄兔腳撲朔，雌兔眼迷離；雙兔傍地走，安能
辨我是雄雌？

沈佺期　Shen Chuanqi
雜詩　p.14
聞道黃龍戍，頻年不解兵，可憐閨裡月，常在漢家營。
少婦今春意，良人昨夜情，誰能將旗鼓，一為取龍城。

賀知章　He Zhizhang
回鄉偶書　p.14
少小離家老大回，鄉音無改鬢毛衰。兒童相見不相識，
笑問客從何處來。

詠柳　p.14
碧玉妝成一樹高，萬條垂下綠絲絛。不知細葉誰裁出，
二月春風似剪刀。

陳子昂 Chen Ziang

登幽州台　　p.15
前不見古人，後不見來者。念天地之悠悠，獨愴然而下淚。

張九齡 **Zhang Jiuling**
無題，其二　　p.15
蘭葉春葳蕤，桂華秋皎潔。欣欣此生意，自爾為佳節。
誰知林棲者，聞風坐相悅。草木有本心，何求美人折。

無題，其四　　p.15
江南有丹橘，經冬猶綠林；豈伊地氣暖，自有歲寒心。
可以薦嘉客，奈何阻重深！運命惟所遇，循環不可尋。
徒言樹桃李，此木豈無陰。

望月懷遠　　p.16
海上生明月，天涯共此時。情人怨遙夜，竟夕起相思。
滅燭憐光滿，披衣覺露滋。不堪盈手贈，還寢夢佳期。

王之渙 **Wang Zhihuan**
出塞　　p.16
黃河遠上白雲間，一片孤城萬仞山。羌笛何須怨楊柳，
春風不度玉門關。

登鸛雀樓　　p.17
白日依山盡，黃河入海流。欲窮千里目，更上一層樓。

孟浩然 **Meng Haoran**
宴梅道士山房　　p.17
林臥愁春盡，搴帷覽物華。忽逢青鳥使，邀入赤松家，
丹竈初開火，仙桃正發花。童顏若可駐，何惜醉流霞。

早寒有懷　　p.17
木落雁南度，北風江上寒。我家襄水曲，遙隔楚雲端。

鄉淚客中盡，孤帆天際看。迷津欲有問，平海夕漫漫。

夏日南亭懷辛大 　　p.18
山光忽西落，池月漸東上。散髮乘夕涼，開軒臥閑躺。
苛風送香氣，竹露滴清響。欲取鳴琴彈，恨無知音賞，
感此懷故人，中宵勞夢想。

宿桐廬江寄廣陵舊游 　　p.18
山暝聽猿愁，滄江急夜流。風鳴兩岸葉，月照一孤舟。
建德非吾土，維揚憶舊遊。還將兩行淚，遙寄海西頭。

宿建德江 　　p.18
移舟泊煙渚，日暮客愁新。野曠天底樹，　江清月近人。

與諸子登峴山 　　p.19
人事有代謝，往來成古今。江山留勝跡，我輩復登臨。
水落魚梁淺，天寒夢澤深。羊公碑宇在，讀罷淚沾襟。

秋登蘭山寄張五 　　p.19
北山白雲裡，隱者自怡悅。相望始登高，心隨雁飛滅。
愁因薄暮起，興是清秋發。時見歸村人，沙行渡頭歇。
天邊樹若薺，江畔洲如月。何當載酒來，共醉重陽節？

歲暮歸南山 　　p.19
北闕休上書，南山歸敝廬。不才明主棄，多病故人疏。
白髮催年老，青陽逼歲除。永懷愁不寐，松月夜窗虛。

過故人莊 　　p.20
故人具雞黍，邀我至田家。綠樹村邊合，青山郭外斜。
開軒面場圃，把酒話桑麻。待到重陽日，還來就菊花。

留別王維 　　p.20
寂寂竟何待，朝朝空自歸，欲尋芳草去，惜與古人違。
當路誰相假？知音世所稀。祇應守寂寞，還掩故園扉。

望洞庭湖贈張丞相　　p.21
八月湖水平，涵虛混太清。氣蒸雲夢澤，波撼岳陽城。
欲濟無舟楫，端居恥聖明。坐觀垂釣者，空有羨魚情。

春曉　　p.21
春眠不覺曉，處處聞啼鳥。夜來風雨聲，花落知多少。

秦中寄遠上人　　p.21
一邱常欲臥，三徑苦無資。北土非吾願，東床懷我師。
黃金燃桂盡，壯志逐年衰。日夕涼風至，聞蟬但益悲。

王昌齡　Wang Changling
長信怨　　p.22
奉掃平明金殿開。暫把團扇共徘徊。玉顏不及寒鴉色，
猶帶昭陽日影來。

塞外曲　　p.22
蟬鳴空桑林，八月蕭關道。出塞復入塞，處處黃蘆草。
從來幽并客，皆共塵沙老；莫學游俠兒，矜誇紫騮好。

出塞　　p.22
秦時明月漢時關，萬里長征人未還；但使龍城飛將在，
不教胡馬渡陰山。

塞下曲　　p.23
飲馬渡秋水，水寒風似刀。平沙日未沒，黯黯見臨洮。
昔日長城戰，咸言意氣高。黃塵足今古，白骨亂蓬蒿。

王維　Wang Wei
秋夜曲　　p.23
桂魄初生秋露微，輕羅已薄未更衣。銀箏夜久殷勤弄，
心怯空房不忍歸。

鳥鳴澗　　p.23
人閒桂花落，夜靜春山空。月出驚山鳥，時鳴春澗中。

鹿柴　　p.24
空山不見人，但聞人語響。返景入深林，復照青苔上。

送別　　p.24
下馬飲君酒，問君何所之？君言不得志，歸臥南山陲。
但去莫復問，白雲無盡時。

芙蓉樓送辛漸　　p.24
寒雨連江夜入吳，平明送客楚山孤；洛陽親友如相問，
一片冰心在玉壺。

青谿　　p.24
言入黃花川，每逐青谿水；隨山將萬轉，趣途無百里。
聲喧亂石中，色靜深松裏。漾漾汎菱荇，澄澄映葭葦。
我心素以閑，清川澹如此。請留盤石上，垂釣將已矣。

竹里館　　p.25
獨坐幽篁里，彈琴復長嘯，深林人不知，明月來相照。

送梓州李使君　　p.25
萬壑樹參天，萬山響杜鵑。山中一夜雨，樹杪百重泉。
漢女輸橦布，巴人訟芋田。文翁翻教授，不敢倚先賢。

終南別業　　p.25
中歲頗好道，晚家南山陲。興來每獨往，勝事空自知。
行到水窮處，坐看雲起時。偶然值林叟，談笑無還期。

相思　　p.26
紅豆生南國，春來發幾枝；勸君多采擷，此物最相思。

酬張少府　　p.26
晚念惟好靜，萬事不關心。自顧無長策，空知返舊林。
松風吹解帶，山月照彈琴；君問窮通理，漁歌入浦深。

送綦毋潛落第還鄉　　p.26
聖代無隱者，英靈盡來歸。遂令東山客，不得顧采薇。
既至金門遠，孰云吾道非。江淮度寒食，京洛縫春衣。
置酒長安道，同心與我違。行當浮桂棹，未幾當落暉。
吾謀適不用，勿謂知音稀。

九月九日憶山東弟兄　　p.27
獨在異鄉為異客，每逢佳節倍思親。遙知兄弟登高處，
徧插茱萸少一人。

漢江臨汎　　p.27
楚塞三湘接，荊門九派通。江流天地外，山色有中無。
郡邑浮前浦，波瀾動遠空。襄陽好風日，留醉與山翁。

歸嵩山作　　p.28
清川帶長薄，車馬去閑閑，流水如有意，暮禽相與還。
荒城臨古渡，落日滿秋山；迢遞嵩山下，歸來且閉關。

終南山　　p.28
太乙近天都，連山到海隅。白雲廻望合，青靄入看無。
分野中峯變，陰晴眾壑殊。欲投人處宿，隔水問漁夫。

李白 **Li Bai**
宣州謝朓樓餞別校書叔雲　　p.28
棄我去者，昨日之日不可留。亂我心者，今日之日多煩
憂。長風萬里送秋雁，對此可以酣高樓。蓬萊文章建安
骨，中間小謝又清發。俱懷逸興壯思飛，欲上青天攬明
月。抽刀斷水水更流，舉杯銷愁愁更愁。人生在世不稱

129

意，明朝散髮弄扁舟。

將進酒 p.29
君不見，黃河之水天上來，奔流到海不復回？君不見，
高堂明鏡悲白髮，朝如青絲暮成雪？人生得意須盡歡，
莫使金樽空對月。天生我才必有用，千金散盡還復來。
烹羊宰牛且為樂，會須一飲三百杯。岑夫子，丹丘生，
將進酒，杯莫停。與君歌一曲，請君為我側耳聽。鐘鼓
饌玉不足貴，但願長醉不願醒。古來聖賢皆寂寞，惟有
飲者留其名。陳王昔時宴平樂，斗酒十千恣讙謔。主人
何為言少錢？徑須沽取對君酌。五花馬，千金裘。呼兒
將出換美酒，與爾同銷萬古愁。

江上吟 p.30
木蘭之枻沙棠舟，玉簫金管坐兩頭。美酒樽中置千斗，
載妓隨波任去留。仙人有待乘黃鶴，海客無心隨白鷗。
屈平詞賦懸日月，楚王臺榭空山丘。興酣落筆搖五嶽，
詩成笑傲凌滄洲。功名富貴若長此，漢水亦應西北流。

月下獨酌 p.31
花間一壺酒，獨酌無相親；舉杯邀明月，對影成三人。
月既不解飲，影徒隨我身；暫伴月將影，行樂須及春。
我歌月徘徊，我舞影零亂；醒時同交歡，醉後各分散。
永結無情遊，相期邈雲漢。

送孟浩然之廣陵 p.32
故人西辭黃鶴樓，煙花三月下揚州。孤帆遠影碧空盡，
惟見長江天際流。

贈孟浩然 p.32
吾愛孟夫子，風流天下聞，紅顏棄軒冕，白首臥松雲。
醉月頻中聖，迷花不事君。高山安可仰？徒此挹清芬。

下江陵 p.32

朝辭白帝彩雲間，千里江陵一日還；兩岸猿聲啼不住，
輕舟已過萬重山。

古朗月行　　p.32
小時不識月，呼作白玉盤。又疑瑤臺鏡，飛在碧雲端。

關山月　　p.33
明月出天山，滄茫雲海間；長風幾萬里，吹度玉門關
。漢下白登道，胡窺青海灣。由來征戰地，不見有人還
。戍客望邊色，思歸多苦顏；高樓當此夜，嘆息未應閑
。

夜思　　p.33
床前明月光，疑是地上霜。舉頭望明月，低頭思故鄉。

登金陵鳳凰臺　　p.33
鳳凰臺上鳳凰遊，鳳去臺空江自流。吳宮花草埋幽徑，
晉代衣冠成古丘。三山半落青天外，二水中分白鷺洲。
總為浮雲能蔽日，長安不見使人愁。

山中對話　　p.34
問余何意棲碧山，笑而不語心自閑。桃花落水窅然去，
別有天地在人間。

怨情　　p.34
美人捲珠簾，深坐顰蛾眉。但見淚痕濕，不知心恨誰。

春日醉起言志　　p.34
處世若大夢，胡為勞其生。所以終日醉，頹然臥前楹。
覺來盼庭前，一鳥花間鳴。借問此何日，春風語流鶯。
感之欲嘆息，對酒還自傾。浩歌待明月，曲盡已忘情。

送友人入蜀　　p.35
見說蠶叢路，崎嶇不易行。山從人面起，雲傍馬頭生。

芳樹籠秦棧，春流绕蜀城。 升沉應已定，不必問君平。

山中與幽人對酌　　p.35
兩人對酌山花開，一杯一杯復一杯。我醉欲眠卿且去，
明朝有意抱琴來。

清平調，其一　　p.35
雲想衣裳花想容，春風拂檻露華濃；若非群玉山頭見，
會向瑤臺月下逢。

清平調，其二　　p.35
一枝紅艷露凝香，雲雨巫山枉斷腸。借問漢宮誰可似？
可憐飛燕倚新妝。

清平調，其三　　p.36
名花傾國兩相歡，常得君王帶笑看。解識春風無限恨，
沈香亭北倚闌干。

望廬山瀑布　　p.36
日照香爐生紫煙，遙看瀑布掛長川。飛流直下三千尺，
疑是銀河落九天。

訪戴天山道士不遇　　p.36
犬吠水聲中，桃花帶雨濃。樹深時見鹿，溪午不聞鐘。
野竹分青靄，飛泉挂碧峰。無人知所去，愁倚兩三松。

杜甫 Du Fu
登高　　p.36
風急天高猿嘯哀，渚清沙白鳥飛廻。無邊落木蕭蕭下，
不盡長江滾滾來。萬里悲秋常作客，百年多病獨登臺。
艱難苦恨繁霜鬢，潦倒新停濁酒杯。

夢李白，其一　　p.37

死別已吞聲，生別常惻惻。江南瘴癘地，逐客無消息。
故人入我夢，明我長相憶。君今在羅網，何以有羽翼。
恐非平生魂，路遠不可測。魂來楓林青，魂返關山黑。
落月滿屋梁，猶疑照顏色。水深波浪濶，無使蛟龍得。

夢李白，其二　p.38
浮雲終日行，游子久不至。三夜頻夢君，情親見君意。
告歸常局促，苦道來不易。江湖多風波，舟楫恐失墜。
出門搔白首，若負平生志。冠蓋滿京華，斯人獨憔悴。
孰云網恢恢，將老身反累。千秋萬歲名，寂寞身後事。

望嶽　p.38
岱宗夫如何，齊魯青未了。造化鍾神秀，陰陽割昏曉。
盪胸生層雲，決眥入歸鳥。會當凌絕頂，一覽眾山小。

月夜　p.39
今夜鄜州月，閨中只獨看。遙憐小兒女，未解憶長安。
香霧雲鬟溼，清輝玉臂寒。何時倚虛幌？雙照淚痕乾。

初月　p.39
光細弦欲上，影斜輪未安。微升古塞外，已隱暮雲端。
河漢不改色，關山空自寒。庭前有白露，暗滿菊花團。

別房太尉墓　p.40
他鄉復行役，駐馬別孤墳。近淚無乾土，低空有斷雲。
對棋陪謝傅，把劍覓徐君；惟見林花落，鶯啼送客聞。

春望　p.40
國破山河在，城春草木深；感時花濺淚，恨別鳥驚心。
烽火連三月，家書抵萬金，白頭搔更短，渾欲不勝簪。

月夜憶舍弟　p.40
戍鼓斷人行，邊秋一雁聲。露從今夜白，月是故鄉明。
有弟皆分散，無家問死生。寄書長不達，況乃未休兵。

客至　p.41
舍南舍北皆春水，但見群鷗日日來。花徑不曾緣客掃
，蓬門今始為君開。盤飧市遠無兼味，樽酒家貧只舊醅
。肯與鄰翁相對飲，隔籬呼取盡餘杯。

王翰　**Wang Han**
涼州詞　p.41
葡萄美酒夜光杯，欲飲琵琶馬上催。醉臥沙場君莫笑，
古來征戰幾人回？

岑參　**Cen Shen**
與高適薛據登慈恩寺浮圖　p.42
塔勢如湧出，孤高聳天宮。登臨出世界，磴道盤虛空。
突兀壓神州，崢嶸如鬼工；四角礙白日，七層摩蒼穹。
下窺指高鳥，俯聽聞驚風。連山若波濤，奔湊如朝東。
青槐夾馳道。宮館何玲瓏？秋色從西來，蒼然滿關中。
五陵北原上，萬古青濛濛。淨理了可悟，勝因夙所宗。
誓將挂冠去，覺道資無窮。

逢入京使　p.43
故國冬望路漫漫，雙袖龍鍾淚不乾。馬上相逢無紙筆，
憑君傳語報平安。

高適　**Gao Shi**
送李少府貶峽中王少府貶長沙　p.43
嗟君此別意何如？駐馬銜杯問謫居，巫峽啼猿數行淚，
衡陽歸雁幾封書。青楓江上秋帆遠，白帝城邊古木疏。
聖代即今多雨露，暫時分手莫躊躇。

祖詠　**Zu Yong**
終南望餘雪　p.43
終南陰嶺秀，積雪浮雲端，林表明霽色，城中增暮寒。

134

李頎 Li Qi

古意 p.44

男兒事長征，少小幽燕客，賭勝馬蹄下，由來輕七尺；
殺人莫敢前，鬚如蝟毛磔。黃雲隴底白雲飛，未得報恩
不能歸。遼東少婦年十五，慣彈琵琶解歌舞。今為羌笛
去塞聲，使我三軍淚如雨。

送魏萬之京 p.44

朝聞遊子唱離歌，昨夜微霜初度河。鴻雁不堪愁裏聽，
雲山況是客中過。關城曙色催寒近，禦苑砧聲向晚多。
莫是長安行樂處，空令歲月易蹉跎。

盧綸 Lu Lun

送李端 p.45

故關衰草遍，離別正堪悲。路出塞雲外，人歸暮雪時。
少孤為客早，多難識君遲，掩泣空相向，風塵何所期？

韓翃 Han Hong

寒食 p.45

春城無處不飛花，寒食東風禦柳斜；日暮漢宮傳蠟燭，
輕煙散入五侯家。

周酬程延秋夜即事見贈 p.45

長簟迎風早，空城澹月華。星河秋一雁，砧杵夜千家。
節候看應晚，心期臥亦賒。向來吟秀句，不覺已鳴鴉。

綦母潛 Ji Wuqian

春泛若耶溪 p.46

幽意無斷絕，此去隨所偶。晚風吹行舟，花路入溪口；
際夜轉西壑，隔山望南斗；潭煙飛溶溶，林月低向後。
生事且瀰漫，願為持竿叟。

劉長卿 Liu Zhangqing

秋日登吳公台上寺遠眺　p.46
古臺搖落後，秋入望鄉心，野寺來人少，雲峰隔水深。
夕陽依舊壘，寒磬滿空林。惆悵南朝事，長江獨至今。

送靈澈　p.47
蒼蒼竹林間，杳杳鐘聲晚，荷笠帶斜陽，青山獨歸遠。

尋南溪常道士　p.47
一路經行處，莓苔見屐痕。白雲依靜渚，春草閉閑門。
過雨看松色，隨山到水源。溪花與禪意，相對亦忘言。

彈琴　p.47
冷冷七弦上，靜聽松風寒；古調雖自愛，今人多不彈。

餞別王十一南游　p.48
望君煙水闊，揮手淚沾巾。飛鳥沒何處？青山空向人。
長江一帆遠，落日五湖春，誰見汀州上，相思愁白蘋。

新年作　p.48
鄉心新歲切，天畔獨潸然。老至居人下，春歸在客先。
嶺猿同旦暮，江柳共風煙；已似長沙傅，從今又幾年。

元結　Yuan Jie
賊退寺官吏　p.48
昔年逢太平，山林二十年。泉源在庭戶，洞壑當門前。
井稅有長期，日宴猶得眠。忽然遭世變，數歲親戎旃。
今來典斯郡，山夷又紛然。城小賊不屠，人貧傷可憐！
是以陷鄰境，此州獨得全。使臣將王命，豈不如賊焉？
令彼徵斂者，迫之如火煎。誰能絕人命，以作時世賢？
思欲委符節，引竿自刺船，將家就魚麥，歸老江湖邊。

戴叔倫　Dai Shulun
江鄉故人偶集客舍　p.49

天秋月又滿，城闕夜千重。還作江南會，翻疑夢裡逢。
風枝驚暗鵲，露草覆寒蟲。羈旅長堪醉，相留畏曉鐘。

韋應物 Wei Yingwu
夕次盱眙縣　　p.50
落帆逗淮鎮，停舫臨孤驛。浩浩風起波，冥冥日沉夕。
人歸山郭暗，雁下蘆洲白。獨夜憶秦關，聽鐘未眠客。

賦得暮雨送李曹　　p.50
楚江微雨裡，建業暮鐘時。漠漠帆來重，冥冥鳥去遲。
海門深不見，浦樹遠含滋。相送情無限，沾襟比散絲。

滁州西澗　　p.51
獨憐幽草澗邊生，上有黃鸝深樹鳴。春潮帶雨晚來急，
野渡無人舟自橫。

淮上喜會梁州故人　　p.51
江漢曾為客，相逢每醉還。浮雲一別後，流水十年間。
歡笑情如舊，蕭疎鬢已斑。何因北歸去，淮上對秋山。

東郊　　p.51
吏舍跼終年，出郊曠清曙。楊柳散和風，青山澹吾慮。
依叢適自憩，緣澗還復去。微雨靄芳原，春鳩鳴何處？
樂幽心屢止，遵事跡猶遽。終罷斯結廬，慕陶直可庶。

劉眘虛 Liu Shenxu
闕題　　p.52
道由白雲盡，春與清溪長。時有落花至，遠隨流水香。
閑門向山路，深柳讀書堂。幽映每白日，清輝照衣裳。

崔曙 Cui Shu
九日登望仙臺呈劉明府　　p.52
漢文皇帝有高臺，此日登臨曙色開。三晉雲山皆北向，

二陵風雨自東來。關門令尹誰能識，河上仙翁去不囘。
且欲近尋彭澤宰，陶然共醉菊花杯。

崔顥　Cui Hao
行經華陰　p.53
岌嶪太華俯咸京，天外三峯削不成。武帝祠前雲欲散，
仙人掌上雨初晴。河山北枕秦關險，驛路西連漢時平。
借問路旁名利客，何如此處學長生。

黃鶴樓　p.53
昔人已乘黃鶴去，此地空餘黃鶴樓。黃鶴一去不復返，
白雲千載空悠悠。晴川歷歷漢陽樹，芳草萋萋鸚鵡洲；
日暮鄉關何處是？煙波江上使人愁。

張繼　Zhang Ji
楓橋夜泊　p.54
月落烏啼霜滿天，江楓漁火對愁眠，姑蘇城外寒山寺，
夜半鐘聲到客船。

劉禹錫　Liu Yuxi
烏衣巷　p.54
朱雀橋邊野草花，烏衣巷口夕陽斜，舊時王謝堂前燕，
飛入尋常百姓家。

竹枝詞　p.54
楊柳青青江水平，聞郎江上唱歌聲，冬邊日出西邊雨，
道是無情卻有情。

春詞　p.54
新妝宜面下朱樓，深鎖春光一院愁，行到中庭數花朵，
蜻蜓飛上玉搔頭。

白居易　Bai Juyi

漢皇重色思傾國，禦宇多年求不得。楊家有女初長成，
養在深閨人未識。天生麗質難自棄，一朝選在君王側。
回頭一笑百媚生，六宮粉黛無顏色。春寒賜浴華清池，
溫泉水滑洗凝脂。侍兒扶起嬌無力，始是新承恩澤時。
雲鬢花顏金步搖，芙蓉帳暖度春宵。春宵苦短日高起，
從此君王不早朝。承歡侍宴無閑暇，春從春遊夜專夜。
後宮佳麗三千人，三千寵愛在一身。金屋妝成嬌侍夜，
玉樓宴罷醉和春。姊妹兄弟皆列士，可憐光彩生門戶。
遂令天下父母心，不重生男重生女。驪宮高處入青雲，
仙樂風飄處處聞。緩歌慢舞凝絲竹，盡日君王看不足。
漁陽鼙鼓動地來，驚破霓裳羽衣曲。九重城闕煙塵生，
千乘萬騎西南行。翠華搖搖行復止，西出都門百餘里。
六軍不發無奈何，苑轉蛾眉馬前死。花鈿委地無人收，
翠翹金雀玉搔頭。君王掩面救不得，回看血淚相和流。
黃埃散漫風簫索，雲棧縈紆登劍閣。峨嵋山下少人行，
旌旗無光日色薄。蜀江水碧蜀山青，聖主朝朝暮暮情。
行宮見月傷心色，夜雨聞鈴腸斷聲。天旋地轉迴龍馭，
到此躊躇不能去。馬嵬坡下泥土中，不見玉顏空死處。
君臣相顧盡沾衣，東望都門信馬歸。歸來池苑皆依舊，
太液芙蓉未央柳；芙蓉如面柳如眉，對此如何不淚垂？
春風桃李花開日，秋雨梧桐葉落時。西宮南內多秋草，
落葉滿階紅不掃。梨園子弟白髮新，椒房阿監青娥老。
夕殿螢飛思悄然，孤燈挑盡未成眠。遲遲鐘鼓初長夜，
耿耿星河欲曙天。鴛鴦瓦冷霜華重，翡翠衾寒誰與共？
悠悠生死別經年，魂魄不曾來入夢。臨邛道士鴻都客，
能以精誠致魂魄。為感君王輾轉思，遂教方士殷勤覓。
排空馭氣奔如電，升天入地求之徧。上窮碧落下黃泉，
兩處茫茫皆不見。忽聞海上有仙山，山在虛無縹緲間。
樓閣玲瓏五雲起，其中綽約多仙子。中有一人字太眞，
雪膚花貌參差是。金闕西廂叩玉扃，轉教小玉報雙成。
聞道漢家天子使，九華帳裏夢魂驚。攬衣推枕起徘徊，
珠箔銀屏逦邐開。雲髻半偏新睡覺，花冠不整下堂來。

風吹仙袂飄飄舉，　猶似霓裳羽衣舞。　玉容寂寞淚闌干，
梨花一枝春帶雨。　含情凝睇謝君王，　一別音容兩渺茫。
昭陽殿裏恩愛絕，　蓬萊宮中日月長。　囬頭下望人寰處，
不見長安見塵霧。　唯將舊物表深情，　鈿合金釵寄將處。
釵留一股合一扇，　釵擘黃金合分鈿。　但教心似金鈿堅，
天上人間會相見。　臨別殷勤重寄詞，　詞中有誓兩心知。
七月七日長生殿，　夜半無人私語時。　在天願作比翼鳥，
在地願為連理枝。　天長地久有時盡，　此恨綿綿無絕期。

柳宗元 Liu Zongyuan

溪居　p.60

久為簪組束，　幸此南夷謫。　閑依農圃隣，　偶似山林客。
曉耕翻露草，　夜榜響溪石。　來往不逢人，　長歌楚天碧。

秋曉行南股谷經荒村　　p.60

杪秋霜露重，　晨起行幽谷。　黃葉覆溪橋，　荒村唯古木。
寒花疎寂歷，　幽泉微斷續。　機心久已忘，　何事驚麋鹿。

江雪　　p.60

千山鳥飛絕，　萬徑人蹤滅，　孤舟簑笠翁，　獨釣寒江雪。

元稹 Yuan Zhen

遣悲懷，其一　　p.61

謝公最小偏憐女，　自嫁黔婁百事乖。　顧我無衣搜藎篋，
泥他沽酒拔金釵。　野蔬充膳甘長藿，　落葉添薪仰古槐。
今日俸錢過十萬，　與君營奠復營齋。

遣悲懷，其二　　p.61

昔日戲言身後事，　今朝卻到眼前來。　衣裳已施行看盡，
針線猶存未忍開。　尚想舊情憐婢僕，　也曾因夢送錢財。
誠知此恨人人有，　貧賤夫妻百事哀。

遣悲懷，其三　　p.62

閑坐悲君亦自悲，百年都是幾多時。鄧攸無子尋知命，
潘岳悼亡猶費詞。同穴窅冥何所望，他生緣會更難期。
唯將終夜長開眼，報答平生未展眉。

賈島 Jia Dao
尋隱者不遇　　p.62
松下問童子。言師採藥去。只在此山中，雲深不知處。

李紳 Li Shen
古風　　p.63
春種一粒粟，秋收萬顆子。四海無閑田，農夫猶餓死。
鋤禾日當午，汗滴禾下土。誰知盤中餐，粒粒皆辛苦。

崔護 Cui Hu
題都城南莊　　p.63
去年今日此門中，人面桃花相映紅。人面不知何處去，
桃花依舊笑東風。

李涉 Li She
登山　　p.63
終日昏昏醉夢間，忽聞春盡強登山。因過竹院逢僧話，
又得浮生半日閑。

朱慶餘 Zhu Qingyu
近試上張水部　　p.64
洞房昨夜停紅燭，待曉堂上拜舅姑。妝罷低聲問夫婿：
畫眉深淺入時無？

宮中詞　　p.64
寂寂花時閉院門，美人相並立瓊軒；含情欲說宮中事，
鸚鵡前頭不敢言。

李益 Li Yi
喜見外弟又言別　　p.65

十年離亂後，長大一相逢；問姓驚初見，稱名憶舊容。
別來滄海事，語罷暮天鐘。明日巴陵道，秋山又幾重。

夜上受降城聞笛　　p.65
廻樂峯前沙似雪，受降城外月如霜；不知何處吹蘆管，
一夜征人盡望鄉。

劉方平　Liu Fangping
春怨　　p.65
紗窗日落漸黃昏，金屋無人見淚痕；寂寞空庭春欲晚，
梨花滿地不開門。

柳中庸　Liu Zhongyong
征人怨　　p.66
崴崴金河復玉關，朝朝馬策與刀環；三春白雪歸青冢，
萬里黃河繞黑山。

張祜　Zhang Hu
集靈臺，其一　　p.66
月光斜照集靈台，紅樹花迎曉露開，昨夜上皇新授籙，
太真含笑入簾來。

集靈臺，其二　　p.66
虢國夫人承主恩，平明騎馬入宮門，卻嫌脂粉污顏色，
淡掃蛾眉朝至尊。

贈內人　　p.67
禁門宮樹月痕過，媚眼微看宿鷺巢，斜拔玉釵燈影畔，
剔開紅焰救飛蛾。

題金陵渡　　p.67
金陵津渡小山樓，一宿行人自可愁，潮落夜江斜月裡，
兩三星火是瓜州。

杜秋娘　Du Qiuniang
金縷衣　p.67
勸君莫惜金縷衣，勸君惜取少年時，花開堪折直須折，
莫待無花空折枝。

杜牧　Du Mu
秋夕　p.67
銀燭秋光冷畫屏，輕羅小扇撲流螢；天階夜色涼如水，
坐看牽牛織女星。

遣懷　p.68
落魄江湖載酒行，楚腰纖細掌中輕；十年一覺揚州夢，
贏得青樓薄倖名。

贈別，其一　p.68
娉娉嫋嫋十三餘，豆蔻梢頭二月初，春風十里揚州路，
捲上珠簾總不如。

贈別，其二　p.68
多情卻似總無情，唯覺樽前笑不成。蠟燭有心還惜別，
替人垂淚到天明。

將赴吳興登樂遊原　p.68
清時有味是無能，閑愛孤雲靜愛僧；欲把一麾江海去，
樂遊原上望昭陵。

九月齊山登高　p.69
江涵秋影雁初飛，與客攜壺上翠薇。塵世難逢開口笑，
菊花須插滿頭歸。但將酩酊酬佳節，不用登臨怨落輝。
古往今來只如此，牛山何必獨沾衣。

寄揚州韓判官　p.69
青山隱隱水迢迢，秋盡江南草未凋，二十四橋明月夜，
玉人何處教吹簫？

泊秦淮　p.69
煙籠寒水月籠沙。夜泊秦淮近酒家；商女不知亡國恨，隔江猶唱後庭花。

題烏江寺　p.69
勝敗兵家事不期，包羞忍恥是男兒。江東子弟多才俊，卷土重來未可知。

赤壁　p.70
折戟沈沙鐵未消，自將磨洗認前朝；東風不與周郎便，銅雀春深鎖二喬。

溫亭筠　Wen Tingyun
瑤瑟怨　p.70
冰簟銀床夢不成，碧天如水夜雲樓。雁聲遠過瀟湘去，十二樓中月自明。

利州南渡　p.70
澹然空水對斜暉，曲島蒼茫接翠微。波上馬嘶看棹去，柳邊人歇待船歸。數叢沙草群鷗散，萬頃江田一鷺飛。誰解乘舟尋范蠡？五湖煙水獨忘機。

蘇武廟　p.71
蘇武魂銷漢使前，古祠高樹兩茫然。雲邊雁斷胡天月，隴上羊歸塞草煙。迴日樓臺非甲帳，去時冠劍是丁年。茂陵不見封侯印，空向秋波哭逝川。

送人東遊　p.71
荒戍落黃葉，浩然離故關，高風漢陽渡，初日郢門山。江上幾人在？天涯孤棹還。何當重相見？樽酒慰離顏。

憶江南　p.72
梳洗罷，獨倚望江樓，過盡千帆皆不是，斜暉脈脈水悠

144

悠，腸斷白蘋洲。

李商隱 Li Shangyin
錦瑟　　p.72
錦瑟無端五十弦，一弦一柱憶華年。莊生曉夢迷蝴蝶，
望帝春心化杜鵑。滄海月明珠有淚，藍田日暖玉生煙。
此情可待成追憶，只是當時已惘然。

北菁蘿　p.73
殘陽西入崦，茅屋訪孤僧。落夜人何在？寒雲路幾層。
獨敲初夜磬，閑倚一枝籐。世界微塵裏，吾寧愛與憎。

籌筆驛　p.73
猿鳥猶疑畏簡書，風雲常為護儲胥。徒令上將揮神筆，
終見降王走傳車。管樂有才元不忝，關張無命欲何如。
他年錦里經祠廟，梁父吟成恨有餘。

為有　　p.74
為有雲屏無限嬌，鳳城寒盡怕春宵，無端嫁與金龜婿，
辜負香衾事早朝。

蟬　　p.74
本以高難飽，徒勞恨費聲。五更疏欲斷，一樹碧無情。
薄臣梗猶汎，故園蕪已平。煩君最相警，我亦舉家清。

登樂遊原　p.74
向晚意不適，驅車登古原；夕陽無限好，祇是近黃昏。

寄令狐郎中　　p.75
嵩雲秦樹久離居，雙鯉迢迢一紙書，休問梁園舊賓客，
茂陵風雨病相知。

瑤池　p.75
瑤池阿母綺窗開，黃竹歌聲動地來；八駿日行三萬里，

穆王何事不重來？

嫦娥　p.75
雲母屏風燭影深，長河漸落曉星沉；嫦娥應悔偷靈藥，
碧海青天夜夜心。

無題　p.75
相見時難別亦難，東風無力百花殘。春蠶到死絲方盡，
蠟炬成灰淚始乾。曉鏡但愁雲鬢改，夜吟應覺月光寒。
蓬萊此去無多路，青鳥殷勤為探看。

春雨　p.76
悵臥新春白袷衣，白門寥落意多違。紅樓隔雨相望冷，
珠箔飄燈獨自歸。遠路應悲春晼晚，殘宵猶得夢依稀。
玉璫緘札何猶達？萬里雲羅一雁飛。

隋宮　p.76
乘興南遊不戒嚴，九重誰省諫書函？春風舉國裁宮錦，
半作障泥半作帆。

涼思　p.77
客去波平檻，蟬休露滿枝。永懷當此節，倚立自移時。
北斗兼春遠，南陵寓使遲，天涯占夢數，疑誤有新知。

無題，其一　p.77
昨夜星辰昨夜風，畫樓西畔桂堂東。身無彩鳳雙飛翼，
心有靈犀一點通。隔座送鈎春酒暖，分曹射覆蠟燈紅。
嗟余聽鼓應官去，走馬蘭台類轉蓬。

無題，其二　p.78
颯颯東風細雨來，芙蓉塘外有輕雷。金蟾囓鎖燒香入，
玉虎牽絲汲井廻。賈氏窺簾韓掾少，宓妃留枕魏王才，
春心莫共花爭發，一寸相思一寸灰。

146

無題，其三　　p.78
來是空言去絕縱，月斜樓上五更鐘。夢為遠別啼難喚，
書被催成墨未濃。蠟照半籠金翡翠，麝薰微度繡芙蓉。
劉郎已恨蓬山遠，更隔蓬山一萬重。

風雨　　p.79
悽涼寶劍篇，羈泊欲窮年。黃葉仍風雨，青樓自管弦。
新知遭薄俗，舊好隔良緣。心斷新豐酒，銷愁又幾千。

陳陶　Chen Tao
隴西行　　p.79
誓掃匈奴不顧身，五千貂錦喪胡塵，可憐無定河邊骨，
猶是春閨夢裡人。

韋莊　Wei Zhuang
菏葉杯　　p.79
絕代佳人難得，傾國，花下見無期，一雙愁黛遠山眉，
不忍更思惟。閑掩翠屏金鳳，殘夢，羅幕畫堂空。碧天
無路信難通，惆悵舊房櫳。

金陵圖　　p.80
江雨霏霏江草齊，六朝如夢鳥空啼，無情最是台城柳，
依舊煙籠十里堤。

浣溪沙　　p.80
欲上鞦韆四體慵，擬教人送又心忪，畫堂簾幕月明風。
此夜有情誰不極，隔墻梨雪又玲瓏，玉容憔悴惹微紅。

章臺夜思　　p.80
輕瑟怨遙夜，繞弦風雨哀。孤燈聞楚角，殘月下章臺。
芳草已雲暮，故人殊未來。鄉書不可寄，秋雁又南廻。

浣溪沙　　p.81

夜相思，更漏殘，傷心明月椓欄干，想君思我錦衾寒。
咫尺畫堂深似海，憶來唯把舊書看，幾時攜手入長安。

李頻 Li Pin
渡漢江　　p.81

嶺外音書絕，經冬復立春；近鄉情更怯，不敢問來人。

馬戴 Ma Dai
灞上秋居　　p.81

灞原風雨定，晚見雁行頻。落葉他鄉樹，寒燈獨夜人。
空園白露滴，孤葉野僧鄰。寄臥郊扉久，何年致此身？

楚江懷古　　p.82

露氣寒光集，微陽下楚邱。猿啼洞庭樹，人在木蘭舟。
廣澤生明月，蒼山夾亂流。雲中君不見，竟夕自悲秋。

崔塗 Cui Tu
除夜有感　　p.82

迢遞三巴路，羈危萬里身。亂山殘雪夜，孤獨異鄉人。
漸與骨肉遠，轉於僮僕親。那堪正飄泊，明日歲華新。

孤雁　　p.83

幾行歸去盡，念爾獨何之？暮雨相呼失，寒塘欲下遲。
渚雲低暗渡，關月冷遙隨。未必逢矰繳，孤飛自可疑。

杜荀鶴 Du Xinhe
春宮怨　　p.83

早被嬋娟誤，欲妝臨鏡慵。承恩不在貌，教妾若為容？
風暖鳥聲碎，日高花影重，年年越溪女，日憶采芙蓉。

韓偓 Han Wu
已涼　　p.83

碧闌干外繡簾垂，猩色屏風畫折枝；八尺龍鬚方錦褥，
已涼天氣未寒時。

148

秦韜玉 **Qin Taoyu**
貧女　　p.84
蓬門未識綺羅香，擬托良媒益自傷。誰愛風流高格調，
共憐時世儉梳妝。敢將十指誇鍼巧，不把雙眉鬥畫長。
苦恨年年壓金線，為他人作嫁衣裳。

張喬 **Zhang Qiao**
書邊事　　p.84
調角斷清秋，征人倚戍樓。春風對青冢，白日落梁州。
大漠無兵阻，窮邊有客游。蕃情似此水，長願向南流。

張泌 **Zhang Bi**
寄人　　p.85
別夢依依到謝家，小廊廻合曲闌斜，多情只有春庭月，
猶為離人照落花。

李煜 **Li Yu**
浣溪沙　　p.85
紅日已高三丈透，金爐次第添香獸，紅錦地衣隨步皺。
佳人舞點金釵溜，酒惡時拈花芯嗅，別殿遙聞簫鼓奏。

子夜　　p.86
人生愁恨何能免，消魂獨我情何限。故國夢重歸，覺來
雙淚垂。高樓誰與上？長記秋晴望。往事已成空，還如
一夢中。

長相思　　p.86
一重山，兩重山，山遠天高煙水寒，相思楓葉丹。菊花
開，菊花殘，塞雁高飛人未還，一簾風月閒。

相見歡　　p.86
無言獨上西樓，月如鈎，寂寞梧桐，深院鎖清秋。剪不

149

斷，理還亂。是離愁，別是一般滋味在心頭。

夜鶯啼　p.87
林花謝了春紅，太忽忽，無奈朝來寒雨晚來風。胭脂淚
，雙留醉，幾時重，自是人生長恨水長東。

虞美人　p.87
春花秋月何時了，往事知多少。小樓昨夜又東風，故國
不堪回首月明中。雕闌玉砌應猶在，只是朱顏改。問君
能有多少愁，恰似一江春水向東流。

采桑子　p.88
庭前春逐紅英盡，舞態徘徊，細雨霏微，不放雙眉時暫
開。綠窗冷靜芳英斷，香印成灰，可奈情懷，欲睡朦朧
入夢來。

虞美人　p.88
風廻小院庭蕪綠，柳眼春相續，憑闌干半日獨無言，依
舊竹聲新月似當年。笙歌未散尊前在，燭明香暗畫樓深
，滿鬢清霜殘雪思難任。

浪淘沙　p.88
簾外雨潺潺，春意闌珊，羅衾不耐五更寒，夢裏不知身
是客，一晌貪歡。獨自莫憑闌，無限江山，別時容易見
時難。流水落花春去也，天上人間。

柳永　Liu Yong
鳳栖梧　p.89
獨倚危樓風細細，望極春愁，黯黯生天際。草色煙光殘
照里。無言誰會憑闌意。擬把疏狂圖一醉。對酒當歌，
強樂還無味。衣帶漸寬終不悔，為伊消得人憔悴。

雨淋鈴　p.89

寒蟬悽切。對長亭晚，驟雨初歇。都門悵飲無緒，留戀處，蘭舟催發。執手相看淚眼，竟無語凝噎。念去去，千里煙波，暮靄沉沉楚天闊。多情自古傷離別。更那堪，冷落清秋節。今宵酒醒何處，楊柳岸，曉風殘月。此去經年，應是良辰好景虛設。便縱有，千種風情，更與何人說。

歐陽修 Ouyang Xiu
望江南　　p.90
江南柳，葉小未成陰，人為絲輕那忍折。鶯嫌枝嫩不勝吟，留著待春深。十四五，閑抱琵琶尋，階上簸錢階下走。恁時相見早留心，何況到如今。

浪淘沙　　p.91
把酒祝東風，且共從容，垂楊紫陌洛城東，總是當時攜手處，游遍芳叢。聚散苦匆，此恨無窮，今年花勝去年紅，可惜 明年花更好，知與誰同。

采桑子　　p.91
畫船帶酒西湖好，急管繁絃，玉箋催傳，穩泛平波任醉眠。行雲卻在行舟下，空水澄鮮，俯仰留連，疑是湖中別有天。

畫眉鳥　　p.91
百囀千聲隨意移，山花紅紫樹高低，始知鎖向金籠聽，不及林間自在啼。

蘇軾 Su Shi
臨江仙　　p.92
夜飲東坡醒復醉，歸來髣髴三更，家童鼻息已雷鳴，敲門都不應，倚杖聽江聲。長恨此月非我有，何時忘卻營營，夜闌風靜縠紋平。小舟從此逝，江海寄餘生。

水調歌頭　　p.92

明月幾時有。把酒問青天，未知天上宮闕，今夕是何年
。我欲乘風歸去，唯恐瓊樓玉宇，高處不勝寒。起舞弄
清影，何似在人間。轉朱閣，低綺戶，照無眠，不需有
恨，何事長向別時圓。人有悲歡離合。月有陰晴圓缺，
此事古難全。但願人常久，千里共嬋娟。

赤壁懷古　　p.93
大江東去，浪淘盡，千古風流人物。故壘西邊，人道是
，三國周瑜赤壁。亂石崩雲，驚濤拍岸，捲起千堆雪。
江山如畫，一時多少豪傑。遙想公瑾當年，小喬初嫁了
，雄姿英發。羽扇綸巾，談笑間，檣櫓灰飛煙滅。故國
神遊，多情應笑我，早生華髮。人間如夢，一尊還酹江
月。

定風波　　p.94
莫聽穿林打葉聲，何妨吟嘯且徐行。竹杖芒鞋輕勝馬。
誰怕？一簑煙雨任平生。料峭春風吹酒醒，微冷。山頭
斜照卻相迎。回首向來蕭瑟處，歸去，也無風雨也無晴

蝶戀花　　p.94
花褪殘紅青杏小，燕子飛時，綠水人家遶，枝上柳棉吹
又少，天涯何處無芳草。牆裏秋千牆外道，牆外行人，
牆裏佳人笑，笑漸不聞聲漸悄，多情卻被無情惱。

春宵　　p.95
春宵一刻值千金，花有清香月有陰。歌管樓台聲細細，
鞦韆院落夜沈沈。

江城子　　p.95
十年生死兩茫茫，不思量，自難忘。千里孤墳，何處話
悽涼。縱使相逢應不識，塵滿面，鬢如霜。夜來幽夢忽
還鄉，小軒窗，正梳妝。相見無言，唯有淚千行。料得
年年腸斷處，明月夜，短松崗。

飲湖上初晴後雨　　p.96
水光瀲灩晴方好，　山色空濛雨亦奇。　欲把西湖比西子，
淡妝濃抹總相宜。

題西林壁　　p.96
橫看成嶺側成峰，　遠近高低各不同。　不識廬山真面目，
只緣身在此山中。

秦觀　Qin Guan
鵲橋仙　　p.96
纖雲弄巧，飛星傳恨，銀漢迢迢暗渡。金鳳玉露一相逢
，便勝卻人間無數。柔情似水，佳期如夢，忍顧鵲橋歸
路。兩情若是久長時，又豈在朝朝暮暮。

如夢令　　p.97
遙夜沈沈如水，風緊驛亭深閉，夢破鼠窺鐙。霜送曉寒
侵被，無寐，無寐，門外馬嘶人起。

李清照　Li Qingzhao
點絳唇　　p.97
蹴罷秋千，起來慵整纖纖手。露濃花瘦，薄汗輕衣透。
見有人來，韈剗金釵溜，和羞走。倚門回首，卻把青梅
嗅。

醉花陰　　p.98
薄霧濃雲愁永晝，瑞腦銷金獸。佳節又重陽，玉枕紗幮
，午夜涼初透。東籬把酒黃昏後，有暗香盈袖。莫道不
銷魂，簾捲西風，人比黃花瘦。

減字木蘭花　　p.98
賣花擔上，買得一枝春欲發。淚點輕勻，猶帶彤霞曉露
痕。怕郎猜道：奴面不如花面好；雲鬢斜簪，徒要叫郎
比並看。

聲聲慢　　p.99
尋尋覓覓，冷冷清清，悽悽慘慘戚戚。乍暖還寒時候，
最難將息。三杯兩盞淡酒，怎敵他，晚來風急。雁過也
，正傷心，卻是舊時相識。滿地黃花堆積，憔悴損，如
今有誰堪摘？守著窗兒，獨自怎生得黑？梧桐更兼細雨
，到黃昏，點點滴滴。這次第，怎一個愁字了得!

漁家傲　　p.99
天接雲濤連曉霧，星河欲轉千帆舞。彷彿夢魂歸帝所，
聞天語，殷勤問我歸何處？我報路長嗟日暮，學詩謾有
驚人句。九萬里風鵬正舉，風休住，蓬舟吹取三山去。

如夢令，其一　　p.100
當記溪亭日暮，沈醉不知歸路。興盡晚回舟，誤入藕花
深處。爭渡，爭渡，驚起一灘鷗鷺。

如夢令，其二　　p.100
晚夜風疏雨驟，濃睡不消殘酒。試問捲簾人：卻道海棠
依舊。知否？知否？應是綠肥紅瘦。

如夢令，其三　　p.100
誰伴明窗獨坐？我共影兒兩個。燈盡欲眠時，影也把人
拋躲。無奈！無奈！好個悽涼的我。

永遇樂　　p.101
落日溶金，暮雲合璧，人在何處？柳染煙濃，吹梅笛怨
，春意知幾許？元宵佳節，融和天氣，次第豈無風雨？
來相召，香車寶馬，謝他酒朋詩侶。中州盛日，閨門多
暇，記得偏重三五。鋪翠冠兒，撚金雪柳，簇帶爭濟楚
。如今憔悴，風鬟霜鬢，怕見夜間出去。不如向簾兒低
下，聽人笑話。

蝶戀花　　p.102
永夜厭厭歡意少，空夢長安，認取長安道，為報今年春

154

光好，花光月影宜相照。隨意杯盤雖草草，酒美梅酸，恰稱人懷抱。醉裏插花花莫笑，可憐春似人將老。

紅藕香殘玉簟秋，輕解羅裳，獨上蘭舟，雪中誰寄錦書來？雁子回時，月滿西樓。花自飄零水自流，一種相思，兩處閑愁。此情無計可消除，纔下眉頭，又上心頭。

好事近　p.103
風定落花深，簾外擁紅堆雪。長記海棠開後，是傷春時節。酒闌歌罷玉尊空，青缸暗明滅。魂夢不堪幽怨，更一聲鵜鴂。

趙佶 Zhao Ji
宴山亭　p.103
裁翦冰綃，輕疊數重，冷淡胭脂匀注。新樣靚妝，艷溢香融，羞殺芯木宮女。易得凋零，更多少，無情風雨。愁苦。　問院落凄涼，幾番春暮。
憑寄離恨重重，這雙燕何曾，會人言語。天遙地遠，萬水千山，知他故宮何處。怎不思量，除夢裏有時曾去。　無据，和夢也新來不做。

岳飛 Yue Fei
滿江紅　p.104
怒髮衝冠，憑闌處，瀟瀟雨歇。擡望眼，仰天長嘯，壯懷激烈。三十功名塵與土，八千里路雲和月。莫等閑，白了少年頭，空悲切。靖康恥，猶未雪。臣子恨，何時滅？駕長車踏破，賀蘭山缺。壯志饑餐胡虜肉，笑談渴飲匈奴血。待從頭，收拾舊山河，朝天闕。

陸游 Lu You
夜游宮　p.105
雪曉清笳亂起。夢游處，不知何地，鐵騎無聲望似水。想關河，雁門西，青海際。睡覺寒燈裏，漏聲斷，月斜

155

窗紙，自許封候在萬里，有誰知，鬢雖殘，心未死。

漢宮春　p.106
羽箭雕弓，憶呼鷹古壘。截虎平川，吹笳暮歸野帳，雪壓青氈，淋漓醉墨，看龍蛇，飛落蠻箋。人誤許，詩情將略，一時才氣超然。何時又作南來，看重陽藥市，元夕燈山，花時萬人樂處，敧帽垂鞭，聞歌感舊。尚時時，流涕尊前。君記取，封候事在，功名不信由天。

雙頭蓮　p.106
華鬢星星。驚壯志成虛，此身如寄。蕭條病驥。向暗裏，消盡當年豪氣。夢斷故國山川，隔重重煙水。身萬里，舊社凋零，青門俊遊誰記。盡道錦里繁華，嘆宮閑晝永，柴荊添睡，清愁自醉。念此際，付與何人心事。縱有楚杔吳檣，知何時東逝。空悵望，鱠美菰香，秋風又起。

鵲橋仙　p.107
華燈縱博，雕鞍馳射，誰記當時豪舉，酒徒一一取封候，獨去作，江邊漁父。輕舟八尺，低篷三扇，占斷蘋洲煙雨，鏡湖元自閑人。又何必，官家賜與。

鵲橋仙　p.108
茅簷人靜，蓬窗燈暗，春晚連江風雨，林鶯巢燕總無聲，但月夜，常啼杜宇。催成清淚，驚殘孤夢，又揀深枝飛去，故山猶自不堪聽，況半世，飄然羈旅。

示兒　p.108
死去元知萬事空，但悲不見九州同。王師北定中原日，家祭無忘告乃翁。

漁家傲　p.109
東望山陰何處是，往來一萬三千里，寫得家書空滿紙，流清淚，書回已是明年事。寄語紅橋橋下水，扁舟何日

156

尋兄弟，行偏天涯真老矣，愁無寐，鬢絲幾縷風雨中。

鷓鴣天　p.109
家住蒼煙落照間，絲毫塵事不相關，斟殘玉瀣行穿竹，
卷罷黃庭臥看山。　貪嘯傲，任衰殘，不妨隨處一開顏，
元知造物心腸別，老卻英雄次等閑。

詠梅　p.110
驛外斷橋邊，寂寞開無主，已是黃昏獨自愁，更暮風
和雨。　無意苦爭春，一任群芳妒，零落成泥輾作塵，
只有香如故。

舟過樊江憩民家具食　p.110
旅食何妨美蕨薇，夕陽來叩野人扉。蕭蕭短鬢秋初冷，
寂寂空村歲薦飢。　蓼岸刺船驚雁起，煙陂吹笛喚牛歸。
詩情剩向窮途得，蹭蹬人間未必非。

訴衷情　p.110
當年萬里覓封侯，匹馬戎梁州，關河夢斷何處，塵暗舊
貂裘。胡未滅，鬢先秋，淚空流，此生誰料，心在天山
，身老滄州。

辛棄疾　Xin Qiji
青玉案　p.111
東風夜吹花千樹，更吹落，星如雨，寶馬雕車香滿路，
風簫聲動，玉壺光轉。一夜魚龍舞。蛾兒雪柳黃金鏤，
笑語盈盈暗香去。眾裏尋她千百度。驀然回首，那人卻
在，燈火闌柵處。

醜奴兒　p.112
書博山道中壁
少年不識愁滋味，愛上層樓，愛上層樓，為賦新詞強說
愁。而今識盡愁滋味，欲語還休，欲語還休，卻道天涼
好個秋。

157

蔣捷 Jiang Jie
虞美人　　p.112
少年聽雨歌樓上，　紅燭昏羅帳。　壯年聽雨客舟中，
江闊雲低，　斷雁叫西風。　而今聽雨僧廬下，
鬢已星星也，　悲歡離合總無情。　一任階前滴到明。

馬致遠 Ma Jiyuan
天淨沙　　p.113
枯籐老樹昏鴉，　小橋流水人家，　夕陽西下，　斷腸人在天
涯。

管道昇 Guan Daosheng
我儂詞　　p.113
你儂我儂，　忒煞多情。情多處，熱似火。把一塊泥，　撚
一個你，　塑一個我。將咱兩一齊打破，　再撚一個你，再
塑一個我。我泥中有你，　你泥中有我。我與你生同一個
衾，　死同一個槨。

劉效祖 Liu Xiaozu
朝天子　　p.114
惜花，　愛花，　轉眼春光罷，　猛然想起悄冤家，　半晌掉不
下。月底閑情，　枕邊私話，　你如何都當耍，　休誇，　你滑
，　除死甘休罷。

薛論道 Xue Lundao
憤世　　p.114
翻雲覆雨太炎涼，　博利逐名惡戰場，　是非海邊波千丈，
笑藏著劍與鎗，　假慈悲論短說長，　一個個蛇吞象，
一個個兔趕獐，　一個個賣狗懸羊。

好好先生，　其一　　p.115
長共短全不在我，　是和非一任從他，　僅箝著三寸舌，　方
免的一身禍。俺怎肯信口開閤，　諾諾連聲揖讓多，　才入

的時人一伙。

好好先生，其二　　p.115
也休道誰南誰北，　也休說誰是誰非，　閑話時點點頭，
吃緊處妝妝醉，　再不然閉眼合眉，　那樣人兒那樣隨，
快休與磨牙費嘴。

納蘭性德　Nalan Xinde
採桑子　　p.116
而今才道當時錯，心緒淒迷，紅淚偷垂，滿眼春風百事
非。情知此後來無計，強說歡期，一別如斯，落盡梨花
月又西。

浣溪沙　　p.116
誰道飄零不可憐，舊游時節好花天，斷腸人去自經年。
一片暈紅疑著雨，幾絲柔柳乍和煙，倩魂鎖盡夕陽前。

長相思　　p.116
山一程，水一程，身向榆關那畔行，夜深千帳燈。
風一更，雪一更，聒碎鄉心夢不成，故園無此聲。

採桑子　　p.117
誰翻樂府淒涼曲，風也蕭蕭，雨也蕭蕭，瘦盡燈花又一
宵。不知何事縈懷抱，醒也無聊，醉也無聊，夢也何曾
到謝橋。

採桑子　　p.117
明月多情應笑我，笑我如今，孤負春心，獨自閑行獨自
吟。近來怕說當年事，結徧蘭襟，月淺燈深，夢裏雲歸
何處尋。

太常引　　p.118
晚來風起撼花鈴，人在碧山亭，愁裏不堪聽，那更雜泉
聲雨聲。無憑蹤跡，無聊心緒，誰說與多情，夢也不分

明，又何必摧教夢醒。

菩薩蠻　　p.118
驚颷掠地冬將半，解鞍正值昏鴉亂，冰合大河流，茫茫
一片愁。燒痕空極望，鼓角高城上，明日近長安，客心
愁未闌。